Ivarna's

Soulmate Astrology

Volume two

Ivarna Kalinkova

Ivarna's Soulmate Astrology

Volume two

This is the second in the series of Ivarna's Soulmate Astrology. I hope you have enjoyed Volume One, and that you will find this, Volume Two, equally enthralling. If you have not yet read Volume One I recommend you do so.

This volume is more advanced than volume one, yet to appreciate the content you will need only a basic knowledge of astrology, enough to be able to recognize the symbols, houses and aspects on your own natal chart. By the end of it you will have learned a little more of how astrology works, gained a richer understanding of soul mates, and how careful analysis of the birth chart can enhance your perception of relationships.

This book is dedicated to all who have taken the first step and read volume one and found an insight. To all who are encouraged to learn the celestial science of astrology. You may continue the journey, you may not, but I hope you enjoy this next step to an inspired awareness of astrology and of soul mates.

Ivarna Kalinkova

Ivarna's

Soulmate Astrology

Volume two

Ivarna Kalinkova

~ purple inkwell books ~

Copyright © Ivarna Kalinkova 2014

First published 2014 by

Purple Inkwell Books
Lake Cottage, Seaton Delaval.

All Rights Reserved. No part of this book may be reproduced or transmitted in any form or by any means, graphic, electronic, or mechanical, including photocopying, recording, taping, or by any information storage or retrieval system, without permission in writing from the publisher.

The publisher has taken steps to obtain copyright holders permission for data not contained in Ivarna's own files, any omissions brought to our attention will be remedied in future editions.

Editor; Edward Henry
email: editor@purple-inkwell.co.uk
internet: www.purple-inkwell.co.uk

isbn: 978-0-9567454-1-5

About Ivarna, and about this book

Ivarna developed her unique Soulmate readings over many years of birth chart analysis for clients world wide. One of her clients from Japan featured her 'Soulmate Readings' in a book a few years ago, the title translated into English reads 'Meeting your soulmate through first meeting your true self'. When asked the about the book she gave this inspiring reply;

"I wrote of my own experience with you, your Soulmate Reading, to explain that we are soul beings and we decide our life plan including soulmate before we were born. As so many women remain single nowadays in Japan worrying if they have any chance to meet their soulmate. I wanted to assure everyone has got soulmate, but it does not mean that that brings happiness, and most important thing is our spiritual growth and if we know our true desire, our true voice, we live a life which we planned beforehand to develop our spirituality and which we feel fulfilled in deepest level, and I put some exercises to find our true voice."

Since then Ivarna's popularity in Japan has grown steadily and Ivarna's unique style of interpretation now features strongly on Japanese websites and mobile phone dial-up readings. Ivarna's Soulmate Astrology Volume One was first published in Japanese in 2007, and in English in 2010. This is the second in the series.

Contents

Contents 2

Introduction 1

The Chart Wheel 2
Reading The Seventh House 5
Reading The Sixth House 6
The Eighth House Planets 8
Reading The Fifth House 9
Reading The Second House 10

The Sun 11
Loving The Shadow 12

Difficult Karma 18

The Square 22

A Story of Love 33
Chart Analysis Of The Love Story. 38

The Midpoint Moon 41
The Mid Point Moon In Synastry 41
Karmic Love. 42
Loves Trials And Tribulations 44
First House 44
Second House 44
Third House 45
Fourth House 45
Fifth house, ... 45
Sixth house 46
Seventh house 46
Eighth house 46
Ninth house 46
Tenth house 47
Eleventh house. 47
Twelfth house. 48

The Moon's Dark Side 48
Commitment And Lies. 48

Talismans **56**
Jewels Of Love 56

Retrograde Paths **62**
Retrograde Transits; Omens Of The Future 64
Venus Retrograde In The Natal Chart 65

Foreign Affairs. **69**

Not Foreign Enough **73**
How aspects can be deceptive for the beginner 73

Twin Soul **81**
Metaphysical layers 85
The physical or earthly material Body 86
The Etheric or ethereal. 86

Mis-directions **88**

The Ghost Of The Past **88**

Astrological Clues **94**

Of Unrequited Love. **95**

The Sexual Labyrinth **101**

Love And Death **105**

Of Death And Karma **110**

Fated Love **111**
Definition Of Fate 111

Venus Retrograde **114**
Aries, ... 115
Taurus 115

Gemini. 115
Cancer. 115
Leo. 116
Virgo, ... 116
Libra 116
Scorpio 117
Sagittarius 117
Capricorn 117
Aquarius. 118
Pisces 118

The Happy Couple **120**

Changing The Fate Of Love **130**
Can a bad love destiny be changed, and how? 130

Aspects That Deny Love **136**

Karmic Astrology. **140**

The Garden Of Love **145**

Lover's Influence **150**
How will your lover influence your life? 150
First House 153
Second House 153
Third House 154
Fourth House 154
Fifth House 154
Sixth House 154
Seventh House 155
Eighth House 155
Ninth House 155
Tenth House 155
Eleventh House 156
Twelfth House 156
Empty Houses 156
Reversing the Method 156

Portrait Of A Lover. **157**

Introduction

Love is the catalyst that changes your life, your tangled dreams and your worn hopes. It takes something old and builds something new. It can be life's Greatest and grandest Passion. You can be dead inside, all hope expired, then meeting the soul mate can breathe new breath into your being and make you feel again, love again, live again. It is the one love that will remain for eternity within us, it will linger even when the soul mate is gone. It is something beyond words, Poetry is dumb and unable to describe it, Art cannot portray it. When you soul is struck by such love, it is awesomely beautiful, disturbing and sometimes chillingly frightening because something within you knows that nothing will ever be the same again. You have turned some corner, you stand powerless at the gate of eternity. The months that follow become stirred with a deep and subtle sweet excitement that is addictive. Your mind is drawn irresistibly back to him. Your life and all you possess compelled to follow a new path. It can go against your better judgment, it can go against reason, it can go against all a you have ever stood for. The soul mate love can be like the intensely cloying gentle fragrance of a tree that ever draws you back, it is insubstantial yet intoxicating and irresistible

It can put the missing quality in your life, and take you from the cold unhappy shadow into the sun. This is not always a gentle magic. Soul Mate love can sometimes be a hurricane. a flash of lightening, that cuts you to the core, and will never let you go afterwards. It can raise you to the highest heights, or drop you to the lowest depth, and break you irreparably. It can be something more powerful, more shattering, more healing or wounding than any other love. Nothing is the same after it moves through your life. You are not the same, You are altered. The soul mate experience is so many things. But always its a love over shadowed by a sense of destiny.

This book is about Soul Mates, and also about relationships and astrology

The Chart Wheel

In astrology the Natal chart is a symbolic circle of time, or a book of your life. We divide this wheel into different smaller segments called houses, much as in the way a book is separated into chapters, or a building is made into rooms, or staircase comprised of steps. There are twelve of these "houses" in the chart; like a book the whole chart must eventually be read in order to make sense of the story, but we can begin with any chapter..

The eighth celestial house follows the seventh house on the great wheel; The seventh is the house of soul mates. Astrology is an science of symbols and so what turns up in this the eighth house, its events its emotions, its many intricate patterns will follow on from the events of seventh house in real life. The eighth house provide us with clues as to the conditions experienced *after* the marriage, or *after* the soul mate has become solidly established as part of our life. Astrology has secrets and this way of chart reading is just one of them. This technique still connects with the traditional method, and supplements it. The Eighth house as my readers will know is the house of death and reincarnation. Marriage is a kind of rebirth, you become changed by it, it is the doorstep to a new era of your life and the life you had previously ends, death and rebirth within your own life time. The sixth house precedes the seventh and can reveal things about the partners life *before* the marriage to you.

The fifth house is the house of courtship, your mutual courtship. This too is a *before* house, it was once known as the house of love affairs, where as the seventh was always the house of marriage, the fifth house revealed love affairs that did not lead to a formal "marriage". Astrology has to reflect the times, a marriage, co-habitation, or a long term, love affair are the same thing for many people. The chart doesn't change but society does, so lets define the fifth house, as the courtship you have before marriage, and also the past relationships that were not soul mates. The fourth house, is your life before the marriage, the house of your home, parents and family background.

The chart is a wheel, the great wheel of fortune, its spokes are the house cusps, this wheel also turns, in a spiral through time. To read the chart properly we must turn with the wheel. When we first read our way round the chart, the eighth house, house of death follows the seventh and will determine the karma, and in synastry the karma will help determine if the person is your soul mate. When we second time read our way round the chart wheel, the eighth house becomes the period that comes *after* the "marriage" or *after* the establishment of the relationship. The third time we read round the chart the eighth house will tell us the material and money conditions we can expect to have *after* the marriage, for this is the house of the partners income. The fourth time, fifth time, sixth ,seventh and twentieth time will reveal something different from that same house, it will eventually on the final time round the circle of stars, show us how the "marriage" will conclude or end, as this is also a terminal house astrologically.

Each house spans time and space, each house is a chapter in the book of time. We are like arachne the spider, or the fate with her spinning wheel, we weave a silken web, we read round and round the chart, until no more can be read and even this is a magical process. A beginner at this method will go round several times and only glean a few things and then not be able to find more, he will have a short spool of thread, but an experienced astrologer will work round picking up threads of fate at every turn and creating a wondrously detailed cloth. The same beginner will find with practice that he is soon also able to pick up the pattern of fate, and follow it endlessly revealing new turns and relentlessly amazing his clients with his insight into their past and future..

The ninth house is the house of ceremonies it is also the house of legal matters. So this house will reveal the details of your Wedding ceremony if you get married. A church wedding or a civic wedding. Uranus here and there may be something unusual about your wedding ceremony, your dress, your guests. Your way of celebration. This house is both *before* and *after* marriage, it is where the knot of fate is tied together, the house of the soul, a more important house than it seems then. Technically this is the house of travel. If you meet your soul mate at a distance, or you travel with him, or to see him, this usually happens *before* the wedding ceremony happens, but the same house reveals things at different stages in time. This is also the spiritual journey of the relationship. Both after and before the wedding, the ninth is the house of your future" In laws." We go round the circle again and it changes to something else.

Every house in your natal chart will say something about your soul mate and your relationship with him, it is just a question of learning how to read the chart in a certain way and then practicing, and knowledge will come to you. Then you go round and round again picking up every fragment of information fate has dropped into the chart for you. This method of chart reading is not reserved for soul mate astrology, we can read our own life story from birth to death this way, we can read the book of our financial life, our career, our Karma. This is the way we must read all the houses in a chart for every kind of reading. We unwind the skein of destiny. The chart is like a spiral, or like our Russian doll its wisdom goes in layers, one inside the other.

Reading The Seventh House

Planets in the seventh house of the Natal chart, have the greatest effect *after* the relationship has begun. Their consequence and influences are not always visible at the beginning of the relationship, it is as though they have yet to emerge from the celestial waters of space. This can take years. With seventh house Venus the love will grow and deepen with time, because Venus kindles love, while seventh house Saturn means the relationship will cool, or fossilize as time goes on, and duty and responsibility will deepen. With Chiron in this house some pain and tragedy is likely to emerge. The further away from the cusp, the longer it will take these influences to become apparent. The signs also show how your life will change in the years after marriage, If you have Taurus, then your life will become more prosperous secure materially and financially as the marriage goes on, even if there is little sign of that security in the beginning, it will surface later..

Reading The Sixth House

The sixth house precedes the seventh and can tell us something about conditions in your life and the soul mates life *before* the marriage, or before you set up home together. It can show what things in your life influenced the decision to marry, what hinders or delays that decision, or what helps and hastens it. It can tell us if the courtship last a long time or is swift.

For example someone with Capricorn on the sixth house, may be dutiful and work hard. He may have a long or traditional courtship or a lengthy formal engagement. Capricorn is slow. The reasons behind the Capricorn marriage will be practical. Money and material things or absence of them will determine the length of the courtship. This sign is ruled by Saturn a slow moving traditional planet. Saturn rules frugality, limitation, convention, obligations and hard work.

The next step is to examine the ruling planet of the sixth house.

If you had Capricorn on the sixth house and its ruler Saturn in the twelfth, the house of sorrows, there will be infinite delay, an endless engagement and perhaps a parting. I recall a client with this aspect, after a five year romance and living separate lives she pressed her boyfriend to become engaged. In England the purpose of a formal engagement is for people who are not already living together to state the intention to marry and name a wedding day for the betrothal ceremony. It gives the families time to prepare and adjust to this change in their lives. The engagement is celebrated, and the wedding usually takes place within three months to a year. Couples who are living together generally do not have a formal engagement but they may have a wedding. My clients boyfriend still delaying, agreed they wouldn't get engaged but they would, to use his own words, get "engaged to be engaged"!! No date for the formal engagement or wedding was fixed. Saturn always drags its heels. If Saturn was the ruler of the sixth house and is found in the second, the house of wealth and poverty a long engagement or delay in marriage may be because of different financial backgrounds or because the couple cannot afford to marry.

By contrast someone with Aries on the sixth house may have a short engagement. Aries is fast and leaps from courtship to marriage at a gallop, without much of an interval in between. It can go straight from meeting to marriage with no formal engagement at all. When Aries is in the sixth house, its ruler Mars will show more of the sixth house Aries story.

The Eighth House Planets

Venus in the eighth house hungers for passion, sexual undercurrents run through life. The person craves deep enjoyment and can sometimes be deeply jealous too, this will not show until *after* the marriage. While Venus in the sixth house will show events *before* the marriage. The eighth house has its value in that it can show how the soul mate relationship will change over the course of time. Mars works in a similar way in a mans chart in the eighth house to the way Venus works in a woman's.

When the Moon is in the eighth house. Powerful emotions and craving for security, or fear of insecurity, lead to possessiveness in love and to violent quarrels with women and female relatives.

Saturn in the eighth house has a fear or poverty and living in uncongenial places after marriage takes place. A fear of financial loss, this fear is often countered by frugality or by becoming sparing, miserly and so meanness can gradually result further into the relationship. Or depending on the chart, actual poverty after marriage.

Jupiter and Chiron bring something inherited from the past into the marriages future, it may be bad it may be good, but it changes everything.

Pluto in the eighth house makes for power struggles.

Neptune in the eighth means you forget your previous goals and plans, your soul mate seems different to what he was when you met him, your previous hopes and dreams can dissolve and fall apart in this marriage

Mercury has no individual effect he partakes more of the sign he is. He blends things, so your soul mate will take on the color of another character, or the shade of another sign In Sagittarius for example, several years into the marriage the soul mate may turn religious or spiritual, or become a teacher, she may develop a love of the countryside, or horses or politics after the marriage, something Sagittarian will develop, that was not there in the relationship initially.

Reading The Fifth House

The fifth house is your courtship, your engagement ring, wedding ring, and any other betrothal token and items, or wedding jewelry. Not everyone gets married, engaged, or sets up home with their soul mate of course. Much depends on culture, fashion and personal traditions. But all relationship have a series of bonding stages or landmarks, whether they are marked with ceremonies or not. All the houses change their meaning at different stages in time or stages in the love affair, this is the house of sexuality, lost virginity, the consummation of the love between you, you can learn much about your sex life and what kind of lover your soul mate will make from this house. When you read round the circle of the chart yet again then the fifth house becomes the house of baby's and children.

This house will include the influence of any existing and grown up children, so if your older, too old to have children and you have malefic planets here, they may refer to your future relationship with your partners adult children, or his attitudes to your own grown up children. If you are young then the planets and aspects will more likely to refer to future children to the relationship or lack of them.

Reading The Second House

The Second house is the house of money, and it is also your own worth, it is the gift you bring to your soul mate. It can be the dowry, your worldly wealth but it is also the non material things. If for example your second house is Aquarius, and its ruler falls in Cancer or Capricorn. you may bring a painting or works of art, or quilt of many colours to your husbands home, these things are all Aquarian objects, but the real gift you may bring to him in the years after the marriage may be to free him from his family or traditions. If your second house is Sagittarius you might bring a gift of spiritual faith, your religion or beliefs to the marriage, while Capricorn may bring duty and physical or practical skills that will be of benefit to you both.

I will leave you to ponder over the other houses in the chart and how they may be read. This is the best way to learn, it may seem that I am only giving you scraps, like a banquet, where there is so much more to say, or serve up, but that I have missed some things off your plate and left you hungry to know more. And I so very much hope that you do thirst to know more and that this book excites you, interests you, never bores you.

If I seem to throw fragments at you, this is my technique, this is deliberate dear reader, it is meant to teach you to think for yourself, to question and work things out, and draw your own conclusions with the tools and examples I have given to you, by learning this way you will learn thoroughly and creatively, you will make your own discovery's, rather than just cribbing and copying and memorizing meanings without thinking why a thing means that, and wondering what else can it mean. If you learn this way, what you will lean will be unique.

The Sun

Classifying people by their Zodiac sign and sun sign astrology has been reduced to a popular unspecialized level for so long, that the sun is a part of the horoscope that serious astrologers have come to neglect. In the first Volume I looked briefly at the zodiac signs, now lets return to the sun again, swiftly, to see what more this luminary of the zodiac has to say to us.

The sun is the core of our being, the vital spark of life within us.. The place where the sun falls in the chart, shows what the life will be built around. So if the sun sits in the seventh house to some extent the central pitch of life., be it happy or unhappy is destined to be built around the marriage or the partner. If we contrast this to someone whose sun is in the tenth house, their central core of life is their employment, their work becomes more than a job, the job becomes a way of life. When the sun falls in the seventh house, or makes a strong aspect to its cusp. The first impression the client has of that soul mate is that in her estimation he seems to be just like herself. The mirror of her soul. No matter how abysmally different others think he is, or how at odds their characters are, the client will always feels she has found in him, an echo, a similar soul, another self to love. The sun in astrology is the warmth in a cold world. Here at last is someone equal to her, someone worthy enough to love, someone to feel proud of knowing. The light of her life.

The sun in the astrology chart is the self. When the sun is in the seventh house it turns the marriage house towards the self, symbolic of being "married to oneself" or married to ones shadow in the case of the inverted sun.

Loving The Shadow

The sun in your own chart represents what you want to be recognized, respected, or admired for. People with the sun on the ascendant for instance want self respect, recognition in their own life. They are self centered; May dream of fame, or being revered for one thing or another. Those with the sun on the descendant, want to have a marriage, or a boyfriend, or partner who is admired. They may secretly dream of a soul mate who is outstanding or famous. They care what others think and of the impression their relationship gives, it is almost predictable that they will marry someone who others respect or look up to, or be awe struck by. Leos being ruled by the sun also have a little of this in their character too. The sun in the seventh house makes you are too proud to publicly commit to a relationship with anyone lowly or who is reviled or doesn't command the respect and admiration of your peers, family, or your own inner expectations and hopes for long.

Many astrologers think the sun can never be negative. This is almost true but I believe it can be shadowed, it can stand in its own light and occlude or obscure the goodness of that light. I find occasionally people live their sun sign in this inverted way. Perhaps people born evil live the whole of their life with the sun occluded, but for most of us most it is just a shadow on the sun and eventually we throw off the mantle and all the psychological hindrances, handicaps, evils and obstacles fall away. I have called this negative influence of the sun the "Shadow Sun", as far as I know there is no proper astrological name for this phenomena.

When Leos and seventh house sun people take up with a person of ill repute, or a partner so despicable that everyone they know and half the people they don't know would disprove of, they do so for the same psychological reason that most Leos and seventh house sun want someone admirable. To the shadow sun person, the partners notoriety and evil repute have a kind of inverted appeal and inverted respect. The dark admiration of being seen with a notorious gangster for instance, or the thrill of being able to relate to your friends, how you once unknowingly dated or slept with the infamous serial killer, whose eyes were like black windows full of emptiness and something in his voice sent a shiver through you. The Hell's Angel Biker whom your mother disapproved of on sight, The drug Barron, The ex convict, the hard man, the glamorous ex prostitute .The dark choices are made more subtle in the reality of our lives, but stereotypes best illustrate the inverted sun, a shadow sun.

How do you know if your sun is operating in a shadow way, when seeking your soul mate? List the archetypical character traits of your own sun sign, half will be negative, half positive, if your always drawn in fantasy or real life to the shadow half of your own sun sign traits, if all your heroes are anti heroes, if your favorite characters in book are sinister, if your dreams court the dark side. it is likely you seek love in an inverted way. A Leos trait would be to like fame, if he fantasizes about a famous film star lover, this is positive, usual, but if his fantasy are about a notorious lover instead, or a star who always played the bad girl, he is using his shadow sun in the search for love. He is seeking the anti hero, rather than the hero. The daemon, not the angel. So the soul mates darker attractions will be irresistible to him and will admired by him, even if shunned by others, but he will extract the same essence from it. The terrible notoriety will bring the same thrill as the stupendous fame would have done, but in darker way.

The nature of the sun sign determines how you will seek that partner and what you will see in him, when you have found him. In Jungian psychology the Shadow is all the we repress in ourselves and meet but fail to recognize as our own shadow in others. The dark side of the sun in astrology is an apt symbol of the shadow self.

Virgo, for instance is clean, neat fussy, finicky, particular, compassionate, healthy and perfectionist. She will be very exacting in her choice of partner, but with a Shadow Virgo Sun, things invert in different ways, the intrinsically clean Virgo when inverted is not necessarily going to fall for a filthy untidy smelly slut of a man. The neat tidy side of her may find a man who shows no messy emotions, who compartmentalizes his life because he is quite cold regarding her. The invert of the puritanical and virginal side of Virgo, isn't necessarily the promiscuous or sexually unselective Virgo, it can be the emotionally virginal Virgo, who has lived a Luke warm life on the sidelines, or never lived at all, being seduced buy one more worldly wise into a darker world. The healthy hygienic Virgo may discover an unhealthy, toxic or addictive dark side to the relationship, the relationship becomes her life's blood. Dreams of dark anti heroes will come true through a shadow sun, but often in a twisted subtle or unrecognizable way.

Virgo sun, seeks a man who will come up to the high stringent standards she set herself. Virgo is a sign of service, which ever way she uses her sun, the sunny side or the shadow side she will try to make everything perfect for him. If her sun operates in a shadow invert way, the unconditional love and desire to make things perfect may result in her attracting or revering someone who seems to be the antithesis of all she consciously wants. He may be a womanizer, a user, an abuser, someone who breaks all the unwritten but normal " conditions" she expects of love. Virgo shadow sun, doesn't so much seek an anti hero or rebel to admire, but more someone to reform, to perfect, or tame. She seeks to make the bad boy good or to save him from himself. To perfect the relationship.

All Virgos like to help and to improve other peoples lives. The Dark sun Virgo gives help but gets unfairly used and abused. Too many sacrifices are demanded, too much taken for granted by the soul mate. Where as the positive Sun Virgo directs these same Virgoan qualities differently, she wants life to be perfect for both her and her man. So she is giving, she is helpful, no one will do more for love than her, but she doesn't make wasted sacrifices, she seeks love by making herself useful. Her usefulness is paid back by the love and respect given to her. She is used but not abused. She is indispensable superior to the man, more efficient. He relies on her, because she is reliable. There is no dark unhealthy side. Because she seeks the light, she seeks her own virtues in him. A positive Virgo is relied on, loved but not taken advantage of., Virgo is an earth sign, a core of practicality to the positive sign. She is worldly wise, loving but particular and practical. A positive sun Virgo seeks perfection of love, that is Virgos nature, but she does it wisely and she gets the perfect mate.

Most people's lives are a subtle blend of the shadow with the sun. It is seldom as clear cut as a stark line, never black or white, if it were one side or the other, the pattern would be easier to recognize, but its all the subtle shades of grey. The energy of any planet is never utterly negative nor totally positive. The sun is usually positive or mostly positive, but in a minority of cases it becomes a shadow sun. I will not go through all of the zodiac signs in this book. The above sample is enough to illustrate my point.

To learn more for yourself, think of the other eleven signs, their positive traits their darker negative traits how will each search for and find love? How will they love the shadow or invert sun, and how will they love the bright or extrovert sun?

Will Scorpio search and find love by secret methods and in hidden ways?. Will Aries fight and win love wearing their wounds and gains in love like trophies on the wall s of their life.?. Think hard about the signs, for the deepest knowledge and greatest enlightenment always comes from within, A teacher provides clues, so that learning becomes a voyage of discovery and awakes your own inner knowledge. Learning that is done for you, to reproduce like copy book, simply imparts information, it conveys no true knowledge, teaches nothing. This is why you should think about all that you have learned in this book and see what your own singular and intelligent mind can add to it. The sun signs are good for this kind of thought provoking method of learning, because of popular astrology, so much of the essence of them are already within our consciousness, like a soup ready to be stirred and mingled with your own unique knowledge of life.

The influence of the sun is most strongly felt between the ages of 21 and 27. Marriage or a close relationship will always be an important part of the person life when the sun falls in the seventh house or aspecting that house. The sun is less important in analyzing soul mate chart if it does not aspect the seventh house cusp at all or fall in the seventh house.

Difficult Karma

In rare cases, we become involved with a soul mate whose effect on our life is totally devastating. People who commit suicide for the sake of love may not have done so if they had never met that certain person and become involved in an irresistible relationship. There are others whose life lies in ruins in various ways, while if love had never touched those lives they may have remained whole and happy.

Love can be a destructive force, a frightening force. Two souls who have met can have very different agendas. There can also be a history of repeated dark and difficult incarnations, and the two people being brought together once more in this life to learn love each other unconditionally or to change the fate..

The client whose chart is reproduced here, said Love had destroyed her emotionally, her material life was left in shreds and tatters, financially ruined, virtually homeless, the stress had made her ill and so destroyed her physically, and mentally. She was the walking dead.

How can astrology help? A Synastry reading can sometimes predict the outcome of a relationship. It can show future events. For example someone whose Neptune's falls in your second house will drain your money away. Someone whose Chiron conjuncts your Venus, will bring you pain. Someone whose planets aspect the planets in your chart to do with health, will have an effect on your health.

Astrology can fore warn of things to come. The astrologer can advise you in the light of these difficult aspects, but even so a client caught up in the current of love doesn't always have the strength to resist, they may not want to hear the truth, or have the will to heed the warnings.

Karma charts can also help. Often one life is a repeat of a former incarnation,, finding how it ended in a past life can help you change the outcomes in this life and help turn a destroying love into one you can build on ,and draw strength from..

The chart of Minni has Venus in the twelfth house. Venus is the planet of love and the twelfth house, the house of self undoing and sorrow. The twelfth house is also one of the *karmic* houses of astrology. So we know that Minni was destined to come undone through love, and a love that was karmic, or had soul mate elements. Venus is strong by sign, she rules Libra. So Minni has the ability to overcome this challenge. Minni said she wondered if in her past life her lover had been her murderer. She said he had emptied her out, killed everything within her in this life. She felt like suicide, like taking her own life, because she had no life. Then she began to draw strength as love turned to contempt within her, she thought if he'd killed her in a past life, he would have to come back and kill her in this life, she would not do it for him, she came away from the brink of suicide and began to hate with the same intense passion that she had loved.

Chart for Minni

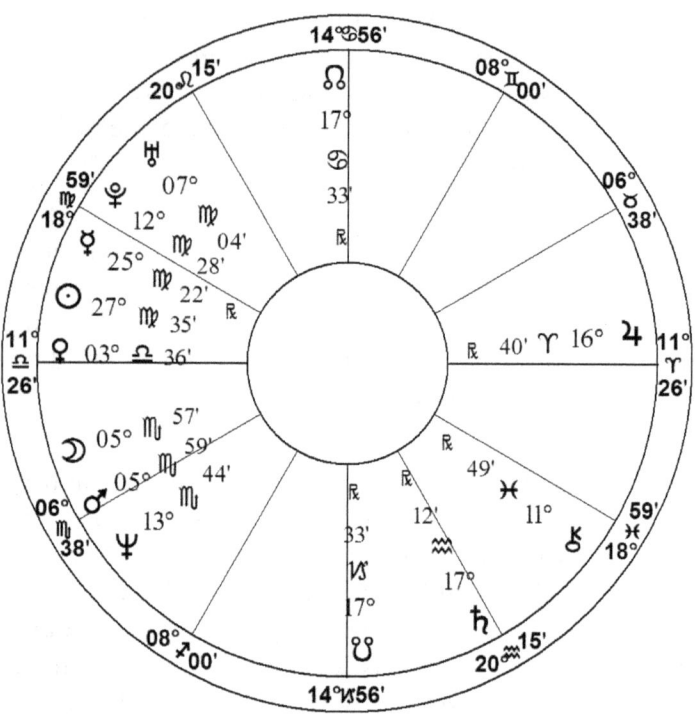

In September 1986. When this difficult involvement brought Minni to the edge of suicide, there was an ominous aspect. This aspect above all else shows how devastating the relationship was, it reflects the horrific truth of Mini's simple words, and casts light on the terrible battle of survival that lies beyond them. The Natal chart is not that of a typical suicide. But at that time in her life, the aspects were so overwhelming it is a wonder she found the strength to survive. The straw she clutched at, the karmic realization that came at the last moment, was enough to turn things around, to transform her love to hate. Hate survived, love would have, and did die. In September 1986 Transit Pluto, was conjunct to transit Venus, and both conjuncted Minis Mars and Moon, opposite her house of death.

The Moon symbolizes emotion, or the soul, for the sun is the body the moon the soul. Pluto is the destroyer. He is stronger than the Moon because he rules the Moons own sign. A love that kills the soul. Mars the other destroyer, and ruler of the seventh house. Venus the planet of love, who also happens to rule her house of death, as well as being situated in her twelfth house at birth bringing the elements of love and death together, Mars and Venus together in a deadly passion.

Minni came to her conclusions about the past life relationship with her lover and herself in a moment of mad despair. Had he really killed her in a past life? Or had she killed him, was that why she had suffered to the brink of death in this life. Or was there some other explanation, had this revelation been a lie, a colorful trick of her unhappy mind that still desperately searched for answers. For all this revelation allowed her to dredge up the strength to survive, she wondered if her thoughts at the time held any truth. She was not really a believer in reincarnation. She hardly knew her own mind anymore. Several years on she said looking back at that time was like looking at a madness.

The ruler of her house of death being in her twelfth house, suggests that she does have subconscious memories of her past life death. These memories, (Venus strong by sign) returned in time in a revelation or realization rather than an actual visual memory but saved her.

The same planet aspecting the eighth house cusp, suggest that in the past life they were lovers, a relationship as passionate and difficult as in this present life. Possibly secret lovers (twelfth house) or lovers who shared some dreadful secret between them. We only have her chart, only half the story. That he had possibly killed her to prevent the relationship or the secret becoming public (Moon conjunct Mars opposite death house). The Moon can be things coming to light.

The Square

What is a square? Most of you will be familiar with squares. An exact square is an angle that is formed when two planets are 90 degrees apart. We usually allow a numbers of degrees out of true, so that if two planets are say 94 degrees apart, we still refer to it as a square. The extra two or three degrees are referred to as an " Orb".. So we might say " Mars and Neptune are in square with an orb of two degrees". Meaning they are 92 degrees apart. Generally whatever the orb we will just say " Square ".

Squares are easy to find visually in the chart because 90 degrees apart is three signs apart. So if Mars is at seven degrees Aries, we count one sign Taurus, two signs Gemini, three signs cancer, and if Neptune is seven degrees cancer, they are in square.

A square is considered hard, it represents a psychological conflict in the personality.

A planet can form a square to a house cusp, making life less harmonious in that house, but the planet while evoking a problem also contains its resolution, for instance Saturn in square to the tenth house cusp, there is difficulty with authority figures and cooperating and working with people.(tenth house conflict) Saturn is solitariness, so there can be great success in being ones own boss (resolution). However when there is such a square the answer may look simple to the astrologer, when your stood facing into a corner, to get out of the room you have to turn round first, but the owner of the square is lost in the fog and cannot turn around, cannot find their way out of the problem., for the problem is within them.

House cusps can also be in "square " with each other. Slightly more complex, a square can from when two planets in aspect, are three houses apart. In many cases this is the same as being three signs or 90 degrees apart, but occasionally because of the different house systems used it isn't, some house systems can have intercepted signs. Another name for a square is " Quartile". But it is never used now. "Quar " means four of the four corners, dividing a chart into four, like cutting a pie on a plate into quarters, the quartile being any slice of that pie.

The basic technicality of astrology can be rather boring, so lets use a human interest story, a question asked by a client and a case history, to demonstrate the full effect of squares in the Natal chart.

> " after all these years I have come to think of you as a friend. Can you tell me the answer to something that haunts me and seems to block me. What is the significance of the square aspects in Rosa's chart which are generally thought of as negative?"

This question was asked by a client whose life has been a complicated web. Over the years we had a long correspondence. His interest in astrology is evident from his letter, Rosa the long standing mistress and soulmate who loved him deeply for many years, has felt disillusioned waiting for him to divorce. At the time when Dan asked this question the relationship appeared to have broken down, irreparably, he flooded her with cards, flowers and letters but there was no contact, no answer from Rosa.. He pondered over her chart for insight, not into the future, but into her mind.

Dan had made the promise to marry Rosa.. He was about to tell his wife he was finally leaving. He packed his suit case, and took it to Rosa's. Knowing that his wife would no longer want him in the house. Then that same week-end, before he even had time to discuss the divorce with his wife, an obstacle beyond anyone's control or imagination arose. Everything was put on hold.

Chart for Rosa

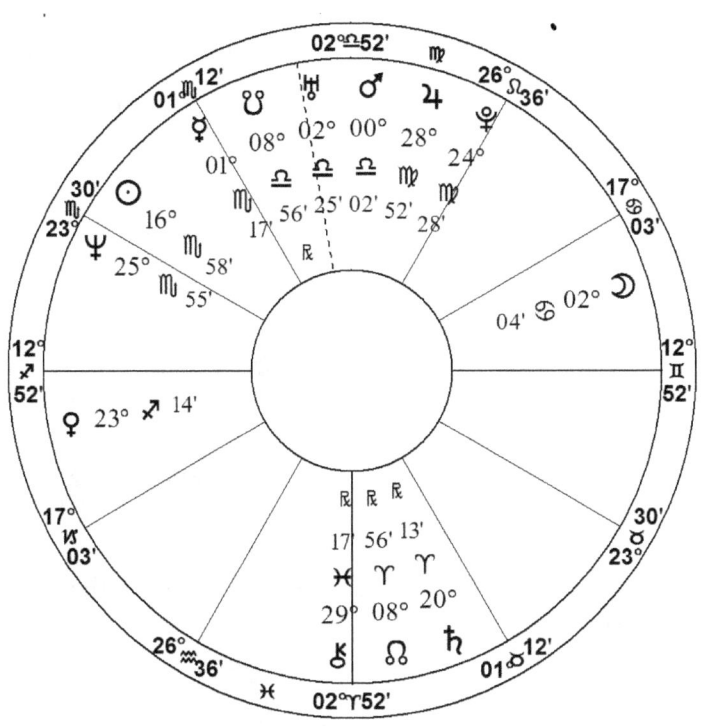

Rosa cannot empathize with Dan's latest problem. For Rosa this was the final delay, Already she has waited too long this time she gave up. Because of her squares, she has a blind spot and cannot see the way forward.

She shuts down, locks him out and closes herself off from her own emotion. She locks him out quite literality as well as emotionally. He sits in his car outside her house, unable to get an answer at her door, but knowing she is inside with the blinds down, the shutters fastened and doors locked. People with squares tend to harm themselves and others and through short sightedness bring out the exact situation they want to avoid. The squares show us the psychological insight into why.

An extract from my reply to Dan.

> " when I found your envelope on the mat I recognized your handwriting and knew you were troubled about Rosa again. Square's can be peculiarly and repeatedly malignant, but they don't *have* to be negative. What they seem to do in my experience is represent a contradiction in the character, or they touch on a deep inner wound from the past in the persons psyche, so that others can find the persons behaviour unreasonable cruel or impossible to understand. A square tends to spew out its evil at the most unexpected time. In this chart the square is between the seventh house Moon and the Mars Uranus conjunction."

The seventh house has to do with serious relationships. It shows Rosa needs to feel more secure (Moon) in this relationship. This security is terribly important to her because of a difficult past and childhood.

According to you, Rosa is " always moody, negative, simpering, tearful, quarrelsome and impatient" (Mars-Uranus, impatient). Not prepared to wait any more so you can be with her, despite her love for you. Uranus is the planet of divorce. So when things don't happen quickly regarding your divorce she fears they never will, she losses faith and becomes convinced they never will. And this brings out the negative side of love. The Moon - Mars, rows, the hurtful scenes. Uranus is separation, and in Rosa's psyche an old wound to do with separations opens up, provoked by her own impatience. It is the opposite of what she wants, the insecurity of being forced to make a new beginning on her own. But psychologically she also wants to get the final ending over with, since she believes its inevitable as day following night.'

Lets look a little closer my friends at Rosa's chart and these square aspects. Uranus, as well as being issues about divorce, and sudden break ups in a relationship can represent disruptive circumstance that are beyond our control, they are in the hands of others or destiny but they rise up with shattering consequences. Rosa feels she has no control, no defense against such things, no security. The Moon in the seventh house in cancer can be childishness, immaturity of character. The event that had intervened and brought things to a halt, when Dan intended to leaving his wife, was that very same weekend his youngest daughter was thrown from her horse and fractured her skull. She was in a coma in hospital, for two weeks her future was unknown, a life that hung in the balance. Dan felt that no one would expect him to walk out on his wife and family in the middle of it all., but Rosa expected him to!. She had an emotional blind spot, a critical immaturity that she couldn't over come. The relationship was blown apart by her anger.

To Dan it had seemed she did not love enough, she was too hard too selfish., demanded ruthlessly, made no allowances, and blamed him for an event that was no ones fault. To Rosa it seemed the opposite, she loved too much. Had waited far too long already.

The other square aspect in her chart is significant. It is between Venus and the Pluto Jupiter conjunction, it has to do with a fear or subconscious memory (Pluto) of a traumatic abandonment. And having to begin a new chapter in life on her own. This is in the ninth house, house of long distance. Rosa is an Albanian now living Uk, we can see echoes of this aspect in her past, She was a refugee who because of war had to abandon her country, her home and her life, or felt abandon by it,. She had to face the difficult task of starting another life alone in a land of strangers.

The Moon Uranus square echoes the earlier broken home and disrupted childhood that Rosa had once told Dan about. A talented child Rosa had begun a private school, but her father up and left in the middle of the night after a family row. There was no money afterwards for her to continue this special education. Her life was ruined, her talent got no other chance. Her father abandon her in a critical years of her life. This personal history was another reason why Rosa did not think it was irrational to expect Dan to walk out the day of his daughters riding accident. Why should he care enough for his daughter to stay. Rosas father hadn't cared. Life goes on. The past left its own deep scars and Rosa hadn't grown up beyond it. This is why she lacked sympathy for the latest delay.

Squares hem you into corner, you face the wall, you cannot quite turn around and face the rest of the room, the rest of your life, they create a blind spot. Let his daughter suffer, let his wife suffer, and all his family, why not, she had suffered when her own father left. Now she was victim again. Having to make another new start alone. The Moon, Uranus square is not at all maternal. Rosa had no children, so in a sense she was still a child emotionally, not a mother. She couldn't fathom the bond between Dan and his children, she only had the memory of her own father as a measure. Neither did she have any empathy with the child whose father, Dan was about to leave home. To Rosa the child was a rival. A square aspect can never quite stand in others peoples shoes. They may have had the same experience but they cannot quite make the transition, they cannot turn the corner and look at it from another persons angle.

We all have a square in our chart somewhere. With a square there is something missing, something not balanced. They hurt, and very deeply, a square is like broken glass, in the chart. it cuts you to ribbons and you bleed, but you cannot quite re arrange the same pieces to see it from a different persons perspective.

Psychologically Pluto squares are where the buried anger or paralyzing fear from back in life is stored, the well that often reaches down to childhood and is forgotten, until long after something stirs the pot again, when we over react with more fury or terror than the situation merits, in Rosa's case, the Pluto anger and pain at her own father.(Jupiter Pluto) abandoning her, reverberated in the fact that Dan had *not* left his daughter at a critical moment. A double hurt at that crucial point he'd chosen his daughter over her.

Both events, her fathers leaving in childhood, and later the refugee experience, the endless insecurity in Rosa history must have left their mark indelibly in her subconscious. Which is why Rosa sees reflected in Dan's relationship with her, other monumental endings and beginnings. This is why her psyche says to her the divorce wont happen now, you'll be abandon, have to move on, begin again. This is what always happens. This is what her past has taught her, abandonment and moving on. That the torturous wait for things or times to change, ends like this. She cannot wait, if its bad she wants its over and done with. She shuts him out. Thus she evokes events that need not happen, the break up, and encompasses her own ruin,.

The saga does not have to end like this if Rosa will be patient. Rosa's Moon trines Mercury the ruler of her marriage house by sign, but squares it by house, since one of her houses is intercepted. This means she can make a square into a trine. She can make a difficult situation into a happy one, it is within her own power. Mercury ruler of her seventh house is the planet of

"Nerves" and is in a difficult degree. It trines the Moon by sign, but not by house. The Moon is emotion. It shows how love frets at her nerves, until she cannot think clearly, Mercury is the thinking, process, the way the mind communicates with us, and he is virtually on a sign cusp, a split mind, pulled this way and that, sometimes she thinks like the square, negatively, sometimes like the trine, through which the situation can be saved. Mercury offers her a choice. The relationships future is in her hands, but because of her squares she cannot see that and is apt to destroy it forever.

Dan took a long time to get to know her, and a longer time to decide that he was right to leave his wife and marry Rosa. Dan's chart is not included, this piece of writing is about squares, not synastry. In the case history I had worked with Dan for several years, long before he met Rosa. Its not love on a whim or a wild affair that will fade. He has more to lose than Rosa. He has a stable though empty marriage and a family. He is dutiful. He is cautious, responsible, and reliable, this is his character. He intends to marry Rosa still. His daughter accident has delayed it, not changed it. He will do his duty for his wife and children. Part of that duty is emotional. He cannot cast them from his life at a moments fancy like a worn out coat, no mater how much Rosa wants him to. Dan did not get married on impulse. How can he leave on a whim, no, he will do it in his own responsible way.

Rosa with her volatile emotions and square aspects, understands insecurity and abandonment and crisis in a different way, she has lived through them, for her Dan's circumstances evoke no sympathy. Squares are hard aspects and the feelings that go with them are hard, with a square you suffer but you survive, and you don't come out more sympathetic to others problems. For her it means she's the one doomed to be abandoned again, so she ends it and locks him out of her life first. Psychologically this is how her squares are making life difficult for her. And bringing about the opposite to what both she and Dan want.

To add a pictorial note for buffs of detail. The crisis that broke Dan and Rosa's relationship was centered round the daughters fall. Animals like objects have planetary significators. Horses are ruled by Jupiter. Uranus with Jupiter in her chart, would represent an Unruly, unpredictable horse. Uranus is mixed colours, but both Mars and Uranus tend towards the colour red. Jupiter towards brown. Pluto is the weakest planet for colour. Pluto by himself would be the colour black, but mingled with other colours it simply darkens the blend. So we would expect the daughters horse to be a beautiful chestnut, perhaps with darker brown legs and underside, since Virgo rules the underside. He may have some dark round his nose, and possibly due to the Venus influence a cream blaze. These planets are in Rosa ninth house, the house of " In laws". Rosa is a mistress, not yet a wife, but if she were married to Dan, the daughter would be an "in law", her step daughter.

A chart reflects the person who owns it, and while some people step children, would appear in the houses of children. Rosa would regard the daughter as an " In law", The moon, Uranus square is not maternal. she is not a family or motherly person. The aspect is a difficult one, so it is unlikely Rosa and any " in laws" would get on. Pluto is in the ninth house, and in war Pluto symbolizes "the enemy". It is a mistake to regard the lovers children, ex wife, or relatives as the enemy. Rosa chart indicates that there will always be contention of one sort or another, when ever Dan's family demands anything, until Rosa can resolve her inner psychological conflict and so find her way out of her corner. Only then can these negative squares become positive.

A Story of Love

Let us continue the book with a Soul Mate love story and both charts ? I will use the clients own words as much as possible, for I think it conveys a better sense of the clients world that way. The names have been changed to preserve the clients anonymity, the story and extracts from a letter written to me have been shortened. The two charts are included for you to looks at. First I will relate the story and then I will go over it bit by bit astrologically, to illustrate how this chapter from life shows in the two charts.

"Dearest Ivarna, It is a special pleasure to write to you now. There was nothing unusual about my birth. My mother was widowed early, I had just begun school, it was my seventh year of life. We lived in Moscow and She worked making officers uniforms in a sewing shop factory in the same State Flats, a Tower block where we lived. The block had its own factory and restaurant, shop and flats all inside the same building. I had a nice childhood and I was happy.

Chart of Annya

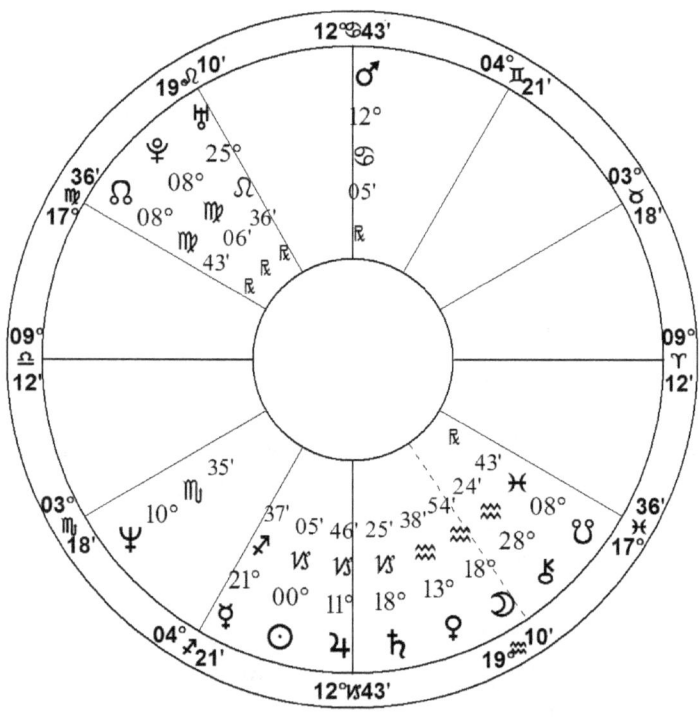

I worked hard and became a professional ballet dancer when I was 18 years old. I did classical ballet, but my spirit was always drawn to the fringes, to Alternative dance, or to bizarre modernistic, expressionist dance Modern art drama. you might call it. Then in 1987 I met my soul mate Axel, at a rehearsal in a small theatre in my home city of Moscow for the Ballet, The

Nutcracker. I had been commissioned to dance the role of the Fairy. Axel had been hired to Tutor the Ballet company and to play the role of Magician in the Ballet.

Axel was 34 years older than I and much more famous.

Chart for Axel

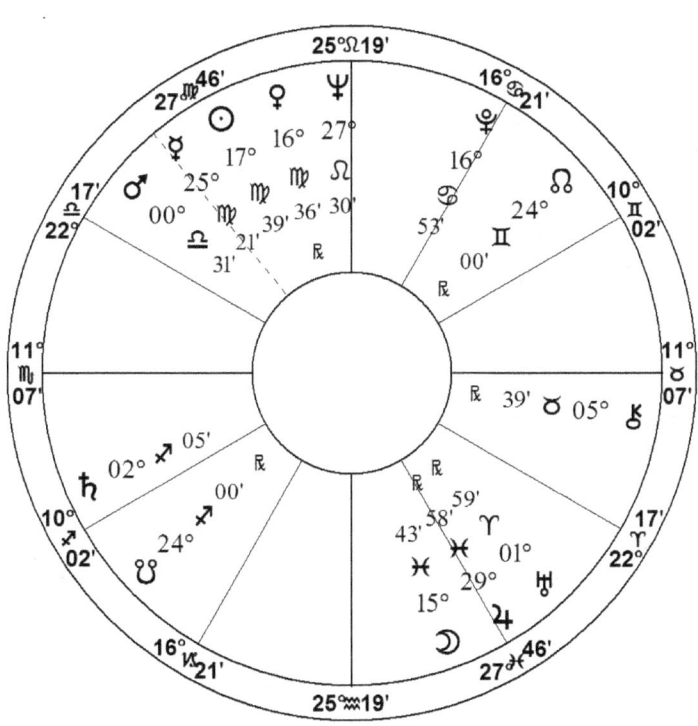

A true master of his art. Dancer, acrobat, puppeteer and mine artist. He proposed marriage to me the second time we were together I was 26 years old when we met. I was contented with my solitude until that moment.

I had always asked deep spiritual questions about life spirit, destiny, the universe and truth.. The perfection of my art as a dancer consumed all of my time and energy. There had been no time for the distractions and illusion of romance in my life. I was a virgin and Love seem to me unreal. Only ballet was real, the whole world was an illusion.

Axel and I were married on a snowy January day in 1989, we laid our wreath on the tomb of the unknown warrior and walked through red square, in keeping with Russian traditions. He was looking for a wife, lover, partner. I was looking for a teacher. A master of Dance. I worshiped the pure Spirit of dance. In each other we found what we were looking for. It took me many months to fall in love with Axel romantically but when I did, I fell hard and my love deepened as we shared more of ourselves and sensibilities. I was his devoted most dedicated student. His constant companion, his greatest Admirer. I believe that why we were soul mates was that we were both desperately drawn to dance, to the mysterious way Spirit and Mood and timing moves in us and through us like a river, in the dance. Our art freed our minds of worldly impulses, when we danced our souls were one with the dance and music. The eternal spirit of true dance that is beyond all words that only a dancer knows." Annya's interest and love for in ballet was only matched by her innate love in spirit, metaphysics.

"I am interested in dancing to learn more about spirit, or interested in spirit to lean more about the dance." We went to live in Prague, we performed and toured the world together. We created our own stage act, which was a mixture of mine, dance, alternative drama, and black theatre. We lived for dance and for each other. Axel died December 12, 2001. My grief was insane and intense. I could not focus my mind or see straight physically. Axel was an alchemist of dance and he was tuned into mystery, our relationship was other worldly, death rent us apart into separate ways. Axel was always tuned into something elusive that stops time but after his death there were unequivocal signs of his continuing spirit in my life."

An interesting side light on this case and karmic cycles is in 2002. Soon after Axels death and during a rare visit to Moscow from her Prague home. The director of the ballet, who did not know Annya's past, but knew she danced, asked her to dance in the same fairy role, same theatre, as when she and Axel had met. Annya did, she wanted or hoped to feel the spirit of the past there, the spirit of Axel, to recapture something. It seemed to her that during the dance, she had come full circle. That Axel was taking her back here. It was if some fate of endings and beginnings of eras, hung once again in the nostalgic air of this small theatre for her. It was this one chance event that caused Annya to ask if she would marry again? "Axel gave me such a profound sense of myself and my beauty as a woman and wife and dancer. He made me feel so wonderful. Because of Axel I experienced a true soul mate in this lifetime and I know what it is to be loved, adored. I never want to settle for less than perfect. But I know perfect is not always easy. And alone is a harder road still. Will I marry again. ?"

Chart Analysis Of The Love Story.

In Annya's chart the art of Ballet so essential and dominant in her life, shows by Mars at midheaven. The midheaven is the career, and achievements in life. Mars in medical astrology rules the muscles, and the head, he is physical strength, agility vitality. He is athletic. Emotionally he is ambition. With Mars at midheaven this is a vital active women. Mars is in cancer, a negative watery feminine sign. Annya is active athletic and ambitious in a totally feminine way, through ballet and the Moon, who rules caner is also in the romantic artistic sign of Aquarius conjunct with Venus, a love of the arts, beauty, grace and vitality in her performance. The trine of Neptune to Mars on her house of earnings and money. Shows success at earning her living this way. Neptune more than any other planet signifies the sinuous subtle elusive beauty of dance.

In Annya's chart the same houses reflect her childhood. The Libra ascendant is the easy uneventful birth. The happy Jupiter in her fourth house. Jupiter and Saturn, the state house flats. The House cusp of the Mother and early childhood is, followed by Saturn, planet of death; The widowed mother. The home becomes a house of death. Her mothers work at there time is reflected in the tenth house usually the fathers domain, but in his absence the falls back to the mother; Cancer the Moons or "mothers" sign, and Mars when read this way as the god of war, in a domestic sign signifies the mothers work of sewing military uniforms for the state.

Mars has a cycle of approximately 26 years. The cycle is not always exact. In the quarter cycle aprox. 6-7 years old, her father died. (Mars in tenth) We don't know if anything happened at the Mars half cycle at 12-13 years. But it would not surprise me if that was when her talent for ballet got its direction, or its first break through When Mars began to reflect her own life, rather than her parents and background. Significantly in her 27th year she met Axel. At Mars half cycle just after her fortieth year he died.

In Axels chart, he was the more experienced the more expert when they met, his Neptune is midheaven, in Leo, Leo is the sign of royalty, he was a prince of dance, you might say. It is also the sign of the actor, the theater, the performing arts. Soul mates tend to unknowingly live parallel lives. The ruler of his mid haven, like hers conjunct Venus. Showing both were " married to their work" before they even met each other. They had a love of their work. A dedication to art. They came together like the lock and the key and opened the door of inspiration, two half's of the same mystery met each other.

So how do the charts fit together?. His Pluto (planet of transformation, conjunct her midheaven. He had the power to transform her career, and the sum total of her life, and he did. His Pluto was in the house of death and reincarnation his own chart. This quality was what Annya tried to capture in her phrase about the feeling of being outside of time and spirit working through them when they danced. It suggested they had danced before in other lives. There is also her Saturn a death planet opposite his Pluto. In her chart it's a midheaven connection, in his an eighth house, between charts. This was a life long dance partnership, even if they had not also married and fallen in love the partnership in dance would have endured beyond time. (so you could say they were career soul mates, business soul mate too. That above all they had come together for that one purpose) Note that the ruler of Annya's marriage house is Mars, the planet on her house of career. A destiny to meet her soul mate through career and for that career to be monumental and central in both their lives.

Her Venus falls in Axels third house, the house of education, house of the student and she was his most devoted student all his life. After his death she will carry on his work with what she learned from him. She is his immortality.

His Venus falls just inside her twelfth house, house of secrets it suggests long ago when they met his love was conceived in secret, and he considered keeping it secret an unrequited love for her, he may have thought he was to old to be of interest to her. But he did speak out and rather quickly. The aspect wasn't quite twelfth house and his stature or position in life (sun conjunct Venus in tenth, gave him confidence to do so. He is a Virgo and Virgos seek perfection. He found it in her. His Mars in her twelfth impulsiveness. His twelfth cusp falls in her first house, his love and also his tuition would rule her life forever.

Her nodes conjunct his Pisces Moon, show a soul mate connection. His node conjunct her sun, showing a soul mate and twin spirit relationship, the nodes are six degree from her sun, hence for her she admired him but it took six months before she fell in love. (six degrees is an approximate measure, it means six months or six weeks or six years. So we could say at eight months she was beginning to feel what he felt, and by ten she did. They were both by then vastly in love with each other and inseparable.

Pluto symbolizes endings and beginnings, a karmic cycle. In Annya's life the story both ends and begins with the same dance. Same Theatre. Same place. In theory Annya is now free to marry again, now that the karmic cycle has ended. In practice with Saturn opposite her Mars, she will cling to the past a long time and find it extremely difficult to move on ,so great a pain, reluctance, and loneliness. There is the potential for her to meet another great love, an he is represented by Jupiter in her chart (Jupiter and Saturn being both opposite Mars, her marriage house ruler)

The Midpoint Moon

The Mid Point Moon In Synastry

What is a Mid Point? A midpoint is an invisible point that falls between two planets. In the horoscope it has an effect on destiny, because it is where the influence of one planet merges with another. The natal chart looks like a wheel, but it is really a globe, and the signs and houses are like the segments of an orange. There are thirty degrees in each astrological sign, and the signs follow each other in a certain regular order. Aries comes first then Taurus and the others follow. If your sun in the first degree of Aries, and your Mars is in the twentieth degree of Aries, then the mid point of the sun and Mars, the place where their powers meets falls half way between at ten degree into Aries. If you sun was in the first degree of Aries and Mars in the last of Taurus, (which means there is sixty degrees, between them) then the mid point between them would fall exactly thirty degrees Aries / zero degree Taurus. Exactly between the two on the cusp between the two signs.

To find the midpoint Moon in Synastry, the path where your Moon and his Moon meet and exert their mutual influence, we use the same method. A example is best. If your Moon is ten Leo and his ten Libra, your mid point Moon is going to be ten Virgo. Many of you will have astrology programs that will calculate the mid pint Moon for you, and any other midpoints, it will usually do a whole, midpoint chart. But not all of your will, which is why I have include this simple method of calculating it by hand. Most will know what the map is but not all. Writing a book is rather like this it must be basic enough for beginners, yet interesting enough for those who know more, so please have patience with the simple things that you already know. As the series of book progresses each one will take you a stage deeper and into a more complex than before.

Karmic Love.

The Moon is the symbol of the soul and spirit, just as the sun is the body and earthly life. The midpoint Moon, which is point derived from her Moon and yours, shows the mutual path of your two souls, and how they are drawn into the relationship or fate between you. If the midpoint Moon in your chart conjuncts the house of death and rebirth, the eighth house. It shows she is the reincarnation of someone you had a soul link with in another life, this is why she has effected you deeply. Possibly a soul mate, or lover from a past life, who has returned in this one. Strangely this aspect can also mean that reflected in his face and features, is something of your own face and features. That may be hard to understand, as its seldom obvious, as no man looks like a woman and no woman like a man. It may be a fleeting facial expression a certain look or nuance that falls like flimsy a curtain over the face and transfigures it from time to time, or a certain stance. But there is in you both, some ghost of a reminder in the physical presence, of him and yourself that has been absorbed from each other through time, and reminds you both of the past life love. This is what subconsciously triggers the very deep impact he has had.

The midpoint Moon falling close to your ascendant or seventh house, can also be the sign of a twin spirit. You will feel that you both love this person and that on some inner level you are him, he is you. You know his thoughts his feelings, and he knows yours without ever a word spoken.

The midpoint of the Moon in the houses and signs reveals the silent emotional communications within a relationship. It is where the storms of the relationship or marriage will begin, if the soul mates are in conflict, and also where the deepest emotions of happiness will merge if they are in harmony. Its house and sign in the two charts, will outline the potential for emotional problems in the relationship, past or future, and disclose what they are about.

Loves Trials And Tribulations
First House

The mid point of the Moon in this house means the root of any problems in the relationship will stem from home or family, personal habits, or from leaving the past behind and getting used to a different way of life. The influence of the partners background and previous family life. The partner may be dependant and immature, too spoiled to adapt easily to married life. Fresh habits have to be learned so this new relationship can flourish. Old character weakness in the self or the partner have to be overcome if the storms and personal insecurity within the relationship are to stop.

Second House

Insecurities about money, debts, differing attitudes, you may feel that you cannot rely on your partner financially. If you are used to being looked after materially it will be difficult learning to be self sufficient and to stand on your own financial feet in the marriage. but until you do, you will feel insecure and uncertain. Financially you may have been looking for a parent, to either keep you and provide for your security, or to indulge you and allow you spend as you wished, or keep your income for yourself, rather than contributing or taking on the adult responsibility of equality and sharing in a marriage.

Third House

There may be uncertainty about settling down, intellectually there are differences. Misunderstandings are likely to occur, not because of difference but because of the way you communicate, you may use words in a different way to him, one partner may be used to talking things out, the other may not. One partner may be subconsciously looking for a friend, or sibling, instead of a husband or wife and so expect to have the same freedoms and social life as when he or she was single or younger.

Fourth House

The partners psychological relationship with the parents, early home or past upbringing is the root of a lot of attitudes that are proving problematic. One of you cannot leave this behind. You or the partner may subconsciously be trying to re create their parents marriage, or its opposite. Thus similar problems and patterns can arise. In such a case if your parents divorced, you are more likely to divorce than to see the problems though.

Fifth house,

The insecurity comes from a partner who seems to take too many chances, gambles, or takes risks with the relationship, and behaves as if still unattached. You may have differing views about children, because one of the partners has never grown up enough to want the responsibility of children, commitment or a regular life. Sexual incompatibility or unfaithfulness may surface at some stage.

Sixth house

One partner wants to follow his or her real desires without much though for the other. The person may want a servant not an equal partner, but will have to learn the difference between domestic duties and the rights of the partner to have the tasks shared. There may be differences over personal hygiene, attitudes to health. The career and marriage needs will clash.

Seventh house

One person is immature, perhaps moody, unable to adapt to the responsibility of adult life. Refuses to grow up in some way. Too much dependency on others outside the marriage for emotional security For example , the husband who is still a son to his mother first and husband to his wife second. Or one who allows his best friends to take precedence over spending time with his wife. Differencing notions about married life and insecurity in the marriage a feeling of taking second place because of this.

Eighth house

There is too much feeling, too many tangled emotions, power struggles, and dark things that take years to come to a head in the relationship. A deep reluctance to change. If the marriage is not adapted to one partner may be unfaithful, because he or she feels too much under the power of the other. Or the problems may be different, karmic and may relate to older lives.

Ninth house

Too much idealism and escapism may ruin the

relationship. One partner will seem full of dreams but unable to make them materialize. The other will get sick of this, and will want more material substance, more practically, less wasted effort. One partner dreams while the other works. One partner study's, writes, plays at life, indulges his or her talent, in the belief it will pay off in the future, while the other grows tired of the hard slog and the unfulfilled promise of a better future. Both partners have to learn to balance creativity and dreams with solid results and work.

Tenth house

Domestic confrontations and rows will occur, it is difficult for you both to keep a proper perspective between high ambitions and home life. One partner will always seem to put his own ambitions first, regardless of the financial, emotional or domestic effect on the marriage. Both partners may find their plans for the future clash, or that they do not want the same things. A classic example of this midpoint is a stage in the marriage where one partner wants to move to the other end of the country to a new place and job and the other doesn't want to leave everything he or she has built up and regards as stable and familiar or permanent.

Eleventh house.

Each partner will want a little more personal freedom than the other may grant each may have a fear of over dependence, possessiveness and money may be difficult focal points. The difference between the love involved in deep friendship and the love involved in marriage may not be recognized and can cause problems if the relationship changes

Twelfth house.

Midpoint Moon in your twelfth house, the root of your insecurity is that the partner can be moody volatile and changeable psychologically, and then withdraws You are in the dark as to what the trigger for this is, so cannot seem to resolve it. The partner cannot be helped emotionally, you may have taken on problems or mental damage done to the partner in the past, which manifest emotionally now. Both partners are easily hurt but lack the ability to speak to each other frankly about the hurtful things in the relationship. Thus they are difficult to discuss and resolve

The Moon's Dark Side
Commitment And Lies.

Of all the star signs, people who have Mars, Venus, or the Moon in the sign of Gemini seem to find it hard to tell the truth and make a final commitment in love. In this section I am going to look at the psychology of commitment and shadow side of the Gemini Moon, in subsequent volumes we will follow the theme of commitments and lies through other Moon and planet signs..

Those with a Gemini Moon like to cram their life with fascinating people and interesting experiences. They flit like night moths from one thing to another and seem unable to devote themselves to anything or anyone more permanently, or wholly. Their circle of friends are drawn from a constantly changing milieu of people, and relationships both begin and end after only a short space of time. They, becoming restless and evasive, the truth slips through their fingers, when they feel trapped or too tied in a relationship, and is replaced with a pocket full of lies. They leave one partner and return to a former one, or they meet some one new before the old love has ended. Ever undecided Moon and Venus Gemini's are slow to settle down and afraid of commitment when young.

The root fear is of the consequences of love or marriage. Usually there is a background where at an impressionable age, age seven to thirteen; there was someone close, a brother, sister, friend or parent has been left alone to face some bad consequence of love and had to live with the aftermath or wreckage. The struggling unmarried mother; The unhappily married friend; Someone suffered loss, entrapment, unwanted children, ruined future, or some other drastic consequence or unwanted responsibility from a relationship.

The person with the Gemini Moon or Venus is afraid it will happen to them. Some Gemini Moons do not believe in marriage at all, but they tell lies rather than say so. They two time. They guard against being rushed or pushed into a future. This Moon is indecisive, evasive and afraid to commit. They get ice feet, They seem to be in love but they punctuate their relationship with phrases like "We are really just friends, nothing more," in order to reassure themselves inwardly they aren't going to be trapped by their increasingly deepening feelings for you!. They aren't going to take the consequence of love going wrong. The Gemini Moon is the liars Moon.

People with a Gemini Moon are attractive, warm, lively, interesting, uncommitted and unemotional, they are talkative, pleasant voiced and always have lot of fascinating things to contribute and stories and anecdotes to relate. They can make the dullest day sound interesting. They have a frequent chest cough, pale moist or sweaty palms and suffer nervous tension. They don't sleep well and don't put on weight easily. They are fickle and fun, fraudulent and untruthful and Its very hard to dislike them. They make excellent companions, but are unreliable and unfaithful. Young at heart, intelligent in mind,, they have the wisdom of the fool, wise and clever, witty, entertaining, playful fun to be. They adapt to changing times and circumstances, always up to date, and they don't make demands. They are not possessive, Gemini Moons can see all sides of a situation so they change their minds very quickly, and have many contradictions in their character. Slow to mature, late to find the true soul mate, a Gemini Moon will usually have a history of several marriages or important relationships. Many Moon Gemini's wont make a commitment until they are in their early thirties. They need love but they need freedom and independence more.

The Gemini Moon is not committed to telling the truth. The pain and deception due to lies in love, and un-kept promises, will cause damage in the relationship and can bring a breaking point in the end. The Moon in all of our charts is symbolic of the psychological journey of development from infancy to maturity. Part of a Gemini Moon's special karmic passage into full maturity is to learn about honoring debts, and commitments, about consequences in love and to learn the courage to be truthful..

By debts I mean what is owed to another person, moral obligations. To some we owe honesty, to some we owe kindness, or duty. If people keep promises or help us, we owe it back to them to repay their help and to keep pledges we made to them in turn. Most of all this Moon has to learn the value of truth. Truth to oneself and truth to others. It is only when the Gemini Moon has not matured emotionally, that it becomes the liars Moon.

It would be short sighted to think marriage or faithfulness is the only kind of commitment in love or the only way modern life should go. Duty in love doesn't always have to follow the prescribed path of our fathers and grandfathers, love doesn't have to last eternally. Though from my experience of my clients a bond of faithfulness, a marriage or living together. The hope that love will indeed last forever is still what most people seek. There are many kinds of commitment, a commitment is only a mutual expectation or agreement in a relationship that must be honored. Other commitments in a relationship are about reliability; about keeping promises made, being truthful, fulfilling obligations.. A man can make a commitment to his mistress, even if he never leaves his marriage, that can be part of the commitment, but it must be mutually agreed, otherwise it is a deception, a false promise that cruelly kindles a hope he will one day leave, when he wont.

There are people bound together by a secret that must always be kept. Others committed to keeping a business going even if the love relationship fails; Obligations to the children; to be honest in money matters; Family commitments and even in divorce mutual expectations of aesthetes and behavior. A commitment can be honoring a promises after death, or honoring the rules of a friendship. Commitments don't have to be conventional but have to be a mutually agreed with the whole of the heart, and stood by. They have to be honest. Most commitments are unspoken, taken for granted in relationship. A silent agreement of love or friendship, as to how each person will treat the other, what is acceptable, what isn't and how the love will progress. This is what Moon Gemini has problems with, they don't want to take the consequences of their action of making another person fall in love with them, or of their own falling. With Gemini Moon there is always a degree of evasiveness, a lack of commitment, small lies are told, small promises not kept. True answers not given and bigger lies build up. The person doesn't like to be pinned down. When they do talk or seem open, often the truth is similarly embellished, or exaggerated in some way.

To overcome the Gemini Moon, in your own or your soul mates chart it helps to understand how this character trait may have materialized. When you know how a thing is unconsciously built up, it is easier to dismantle it consciously.

The Gemini Moon, most especially when in the fourth, tenth or eighth, house, suggests that lying, embellishing the truth or saying one thing then doing another, has become a habit that began a long time ago, possibly originating in childhood. The theme of the prying parent or sibling in his childhood, who would question him, wanted to know everything about him, where he was going, what he was doing. With a Gemini Moon childhood this probing is generally not connected with strictness or disapproval, or discipline, it is not to do with right and wrong and punishments for transgressions usually the parent is genuinely interested and curious about child's life. The parent is open, not secretive and sees no reason for the child to keep things to himself. The parent wants to be included in his life, but by adolescence or early adult years the child finds it invasive. He wants to distance himself form this parent and live his life without an onlooker. He has secrets. Things he doesn't want to share. So he learns to be evasive, non committal, to twist and weave the truth. He lies about little unimportant things. Saying he was visiting one school friend, when he was really visiting another. A lie that would seem pointless and baffling to the parent if found out.! But such lies and evasions are the easiest way for him to deal with intrusion. They create space in his life, and these things tend to become habitual or get built into part of the character.

At the other side of the same psychological balance is that the Gemini Moon child is used to feeling he has an interested audience in the family, and a non hostile one at that, part of him likes certain aspects of that, he learns to display himself to best advantage, to play to the crowd. (first and tenth house Gemini Moon) He learns to exaggerate his successes, to incorporate other little lies, to enhance his reputation, he embellishes, he makes himself seem, more colorful, more interesting, more brave, more the hero, more the centre of things.. In adult years, the Gemini Moon may automatically twist the truth both ways, tell lies, embellish certain things hide other things, become a trickster and live a double life. The twelfth house Gemini Moon, is shy unassertive, he says yes when he means no, seems to be in earnest when he isn't, a split personality.

Gemini Moon in the first, eleventh, fifth or seventh house, has difficulty telling the truth in relationships and committing to them permanently. When the Gemini Moon is in the second house, the early deceptions and need for space and privacy would have been about pocket money possessions, and the family or a parent may have an ambiguous attitude about finances, the one rule for me, another for you, attitude that may have been almost inherited. The child may have asked for money to spend on violin lessons, but spent it on sweets. The adult Gemini Moon asks to borrow for money for one thing, uses it for another..

In the tenth house he will be one person at home another at work. When as a boy at home with his mother he was her good child but when with his friends he was a trouble maker and his own person. Two different people. Two faces. His wife will know him as a devoted husband, the office girls will know him as lecher or flirt. Only when the two lives collide are the discrepancies found out.

We have looked at the Moon child. How does this scenario continue into adult relationships? Men with a Gemini Moon tend to involve themselves with a partner who superficially gives him a lot of independence and space and freedom, A woman who has her own life to live, or is absent a lot. But who is also a curious prying wife when they are together, someone who he is expected to share everything with and tell everything to, in that respect she inadvertently carry's on the parental role. . He in turn will perpetuate the same deceptions founded in the childhood The lying or evading can become more entrenched in marriage

That is the usual passage of the dark side of a Gemini Moon. But just occasionally the reverse happens then the man with the Gemini Moon will be youthful, open trusting and naive, and will attract a wife who is the liar, the cheat, the one who is not constant, never commits, she will be complex person, usually with a sad or victimized past, for a man with a Gemini Moon can mistake pity for love, someone economic with the truth and evasive herself. Someone who will seem to have had a more interesting life than him. He will be attracted to her because his subconscious recognizes something of himself in that pattern and through her he will confront his own childhood pattern of not telling the whole truth, of embroidering stories, and so on of saying they he was one place when he was at another. What we don't confront in ourselves we confront in other people. Gemini moon people often have several marriages. They can deceive or be deceived. Often they get both type of partner but at different times. The cycle repeats like a karma until the Gemini moon evolves enough by life's experiences to conquer the tendency to be untruthful and the fear of commitment and. Then maturity comes, and with it wisdom, fate changes he meets the woman he never lies to and commits himself to totally, in what ever way they decide is a true and mutual commitment for them. This woman of course, the love who knows his true self is his true soul mate.

The lies and frauds and discrepancies of a Gemini Moon, do not always materialize in love, This goes almost without saying, but I feel the need to remind the reader. If they are to do with love, the Gemini Moon will be connected by aspects, usually hard aspects, to the planets and houses to do relationships in the chart. If the Gemini Moon doesn't aspect those areas, then the dark side of Gemini Moon manifest itself in other areas of life, business for example, but this volume is only about soul mate, so I will not stray into other avenues.

Talismans
Jewels Of Love

The making of talismans and amulets to attract a soul mate, was once a specialized and individual process. It was done astrologically. The Natal chart is like a kind of prescription, one can see what metaphysical elements are causing life to go wrong. Just as the body can become out of balance and the person becomes ill, so the spirit can be out of balance and be attracting an unhappy or unlucky state of affairs in life. The chart reflects this subtle balance or energies. The making of a talisman or amulet was an attempt to focus the energies of the planets in a way that would correct the balance, and so if the amulet was made for the purposes of love, it would draw, or preserve and protect love. They were made for many different purposes to attract good fortune, to protect travelers, to brings successes, but each one required a study of the chart. The difference between an Amulet and a Talisman, is an Amulet wards off evil, a talisman attracts good.

The talismans and amulets, were made of natural materials, usually precious and semi precious stone. In modern times this old knowledge has sunk into disuse and into superstition. The "lucky charms" we wear are a remnant of this same ancient art. But jewelry doesn't have to be specially made, or extraordinary to bring happiness love and good fortune, sometimes we chance across certain pieces of jewelry and it is as though they have been sitting waiting for us, they may not be magical in any way but they echo something within us, such a piece will always be lucky

In many countries a wedding ring is made of a gold band sometimes plain, sometimes decorative, ornate or inscribed. Gold is the most precious or valued of metals, and love is the more treasures of gifts. Gold is the metal of the sun, and the sun in astrology is ones life. A modern day suffragette, as she called herself, whose belief is that women have not yet reached true independence told me a wedding ring was symbol of slavery, like an iron manacle, dating back to when a man owned the woman he married, and she was no more than a chattel. That may be so, I Have also heard more Freudian interpretations of the ring and finger, and a circle is always unity, that which encircles, but either way the band of gold, is a symbol of the bondage of love for life, or perhaps longer, for gold was the alchemic symbol of immortality. The third finger of the left hand, where a gold ring is traditionally worn, is the finger which in palmistry and astrology is ruled by the sun, The ring symbolically strengthening and focusing its power of life and love. This is one fragment of the forgotten link of astrology, symbolism and jewels.

There are also certain precious and semi precious stones that are, related to zodiacal signs, their spiritual vibration intensifies the powers of the sign

There is a difference of opinions about which stones are assigned to each sign, but these are what I have found effective. Those related to your zodiac sign will increase your good luck. Wearing or possessing the stone linked to your descendant (seventh house cusp) or your Venus sign, has an ancient power to help attract love, or to strengthen an on going love.

Aries, Zircon, diamond, Amethyst, garnet, ruby pearls. Heliotrope, All sparkling and fiery substances. Sapphires can also bring luck in love to Aries.

Taurus, Jade, emeralds, moss agate, coral, lapis lazuli. Carnelian

Gemini, quarts crystal. Aquamarine, turquoise, beryl, chrisolite. Also veined substances, like marble. Modern, new and fashion jewelry

Cancer, opal, clear quarts, Moon stones, pearl and mother of pearl, emerald, silver and silvery substances.

Leo, gold, Alexandrite, tigers eye, golden amber, Algurite, also glistening or luminescent substances,

Virgo, topaz, aqua marines, agate. Glass, Peridot. Almandine, Amethyst

Libra, cornelian, beryl, copper, red gold, Nephrite, brass, colored glass and substances which reflect light or are highly polished.

Scorpio, malachite, topaz, red amber, all dark murky and mysterious substances. Bohemian glass. Meaningful and mystical or occult jewelry.

Sagittarius, turquoise, Moon stone. Lapis lazuli, Azurite Also common and useful substances. Jewelry of religious significance.

Capricorn, onyx, jet, sapphire, lead. pewter, dark mottled substances. Amber, ammonites, antique jewelry and things of the past.

Aquarius, Alexandrite, sapphire, hematite, amber, slate, electric tones and magnetic substances. Antique jewelry and hand made arts and crafts items.

Pisces, Hyacinth, white gold, shell and coral. Aquamarine, cloudy pearl colored quartz and some opals. Picture stone, sea glass. Blue john.

How do stones exert their mysterious influence? All things in life are connected. The stone or piece of jewelry you choose to bring love and happiness in your life is linked to the eternal connectedness of all things, its own energy re-channels the subtle vibrations of energy around it to attract a karmic healing and balancing, it draws positive elements into life and acts as catalyst and "changes" or transforms or mends our own negative energies, thoughts, subconscious actions and responses, all the things we unknowingly do to obstruct ourselves or to dampen our own luck and prospects. Keep the mystical jewelry or stone with you, a neglected jewel is like a neglected plant, it won't have the vitality and power that a cared for one does.

The semi precious stones are a living rock, in the same way that a plant is alive and has energy. A plant can heal us through herbs and medicines that come from its roots and leaves. A semi precious stone can correct things in our life through its etheric vibration, the way its spiritual vibration mingles with our own. A rock does not respond as visibly as a plant, it is infinitely slow to grow, it doesn't droop or thrive, but it will respond on the vibration or metaphysical level, even if you can not perceive that response. To have faith in something or some process you can neither see nor perceive is not unusual, most religions are based on such. The rocks substance brings a powerful blessing of pure love and unity with the world into your life to and enhances your power, along with the stones natural radiant power.

In an idle moment you may find yourself lost in thought, dreaming of love as both lovers and lonely people do, unconsciously your hands may travel to touch the stone or play with jewelry. This actually recharges the natural power and helps your spirit bond with the spirit of the jewelry. If you should find yourself Caressing your bracelet or pulling at your necklace then you should at the moment put you hearts desire into it, think of your soul mate and of him being drawn to you, think of him with all the love within you that you can summon, this will help focus the energy and will help focus your desires

Occasional cleansing of Jewelry is recommended, but only when it magical effects seem to be diminished or to bring the reverse of what's desired. The cleansing helps recharges and purify the energies, it also allows the vibration of accumulated negative fragments left from what ever the stone has helped you through in life or protected you from to disintegrate and flow away. These fragments of energy can after a while clog up or dull the power.

Retrograde Paths

When we look at the planets from earth, as the ancients did, the normal course of a planet is to seem to move forwards through the signs and houses and the backdrop of the stars.

This journey through the zodiac can take many years, and as the planet aspects or appears to touch others in its path, it inspires events to happen, it cause the energies of the two planets to mingle and unlocks a door of fate, The motion or speed of a planet, and the motion of the earth, from which the planets are viewed is not always the same. Planets including the earth speed up and slow down, this may only be by a second or so in reality. But in a symbolic art like astrology each second is important and has an effect. When a planet seems to stand still in the night sky, instead of moving forwards it is called a Station, and has the effect of blocking that area of life for as long as its stationary. So that nothing moves forwards in ones life. Sometimes the earth will speed up by a second, and this can give the impression of another planet standing still, or moving backwards. Moving backwards is called Retrograde.

The retrograde motion of a planet transiting your chart, can hold its influence in several different ways, First it can delay things. If you waiting for a letter from your love, and transit mercury turns retrograde in your third house you will wait longer, it will be delayed or denied and won't come when you hope it will. A person in who's natal chart the significators of love are retrograde, say Mars, Venus, or the ruler of the seventh house, or if they have a retrograde planet in or aspecting the seventh house at birth, will most likely suffer delay or disappointments before finding a true love. Retrograde slow things down.

Retrogrades move backwards, the other effect of retrograde transits is they turn everything back with them. Sometimes it repeats the same situation and circumstance that happened before, sometimes it gives a second chance in the same relationship, or it brings something unfinished from the past when it made the first aspect, to its final conclusion.

In Synastry or by transit. A retrograde will be fortunate if we are hoping for a return to an old condition, for a reunion or the reinstatement of previous conditions, for the return of a possession or person which has been lost to us. The person signified by the retrograde is likely to withdraw from the relationship. So if the ruler of the seventh house for example is retrograde, by natal or transit, then there will come a point when the partner may withdraw, leave or turn away from the relationship. If the ruler of the first house is retrograde then you yourself will be the one who withdraws the love and support for your partner

A retrograde planet indicates a reluctance to begin, or to make a start in a new direction, old conditions will prevail. Thus someone with a retrograde planet in the fourth house may be reluctant to marry if marriage means leaving the neighborhood, home, or family behind and moving far away, and if they do leave, their heart will always feel compelled to return there, in thought or action or mind set. This will prevent the person settling in their new home and making the best of the new life, the less the new place is like home the greater and more difficult the future adjustment will be, if the person is not willing to make that adjustment it will subconsciously create a negative undercurrent to afflict the marriage. Where ever there is a retrograde planet in a Natal chart there is the root of an old problem.

There is less energy and potential for success in a retrograde planet, less initiative, more inclination to loose, fail, or let the world and opportunities pass by without grasping them, with retrogrades in the seventh love may arrive but it may also slip through your grasp like the seasons of the year.

Retrogrades often have a measure of karma attached to them, so the marriage chart or relationship chart must be carefully studied and the client advised how to overcome the effects of the retrograde. What she must adjust to, and what is holding her back. What she must leave behind.

Retrograde Transits; Omens Of The Future
There is an old rule of astrology that if a slow moving transiting planet retrogrades back into a previous sign and in so doing, makes a good aspect with a planet that has to do with love or with the particular relationship, this will indicate there will soon be a dramatic improvement, or the mending of the relationship.

If the client is anxious about a separation from a partner and the ruler of her first house is retrograde, it is likely that the client will attempt a reconciliation. This is because she will dearly wish to return to past situation, to the way things were. If the ruler of the seventh house, is retrograde than it is more certain she will attempt the reconciliation. If the majority of aspects between the significator are good then reconciliation will likely be successful. But if a retrograde transit aspects the Moon, there may be tears or disappointment in maters of love, and in the other things the Moon in the individual chart signifies.

Venus Retrograde In The Natal Chart

People born in the retrograde cycle of Venus, when her power is dark, always seek a soul mate and with it some kind of hidden meaning or love that's more than love. If you have a retrograde Venus you are looking for something deep, that sifts into the soul, or shatters the material or worldly levels of love and transcends the every day life. For retrograde Venus it is the inner love of the spirit that is important, a retrograde planet is an in turned planet, a planet turned away from the outer world of the material, to the inner realms of experience, and the soul. This Venus can bring disappointment, there is often a vast difference between the dream in their mind and what seems to be their destiny in the world. So they often subconsciously reject ordinary relationships and ordinary people with one excuse or another. A retrograde Venus delays finding happiness in love, or delays finding love.

Men who have a retrograde Mars and women who have

a retrograde Venus have subconscious memories of having known their soul mate. Their lives are often devoid of real love because the spirit seeks the soul mate so strongly that no other relationship can bring happiness or fill the gap in their lives. Even if they are the life and soul of the party or know a million loves, which usually they don't, as they are often introvert with the opposite sex, there is an empty core that nothing can touch.

Retrograde Venus people have an unusual fascination or Interest in Love and relationships. They make good Jungian or Freudian analysts for they always seek something deeper or more obscure, taboo or hidden. But in their private life they have difficulty evoking love and mentally and physically they do not seem to become aroused into love by ordinary means. Retrograde Venus has to do with mental or physical masturbation, the person who creates their own love, or private fantasies, or sublimates it into a dedication to other things work, hobbies, art. Socially they don't fit into the mainstream. Some people with Venus in this condition become asexual or celibate, they are the ice maidens, the snow men. Or occasionally the reverse sexual Celebrants, full of lust and lechery and promiscuities, yet still dissatisfied and still disconnected from love. Sex and love are not the same. How Venus manifests depends on the Venus sign and the rest of the chart. These phases can alternate at various stages in the life between these two opposite, the feast or famine. Adverse or perverse. The retrograde Venus is a Venus turned inward. Idealism about love forms to such a high expectation that no one

Can fill it. The end result is a feeling of a great gulf of loneliness in life of never being loved at all. With a Retrograde Venus. You are different. And you may deny your need for love. You may only marry late in life.

If you do not find the soul mate then you may turn to Spirituality or Religion, because it is easier to love god, or an ideal than humanity. Sometimes a retrograde Venus can be part of an Afflicted chart, where the person has suffered in love or undergone traumatic experiences with those they love. Venus retrograde people do not always make the happiest marriage partners, there can be a barrier there, they sometimes don't really like the opposite sex and they can be at odds with the traditional wedding philosophy, social aspects or traditional roles of marriage. They can prefer their own company or the companionship of their own sex. Venus retrograde has to do with love turned Introspectively and away from the world, Turned either to the self, to spirit, the past, and the unconscious search for the soul mate, or Away from earth to unworldly things and unworldly loves..

With retrograde Venus its as though you dare not seek the love you crave. Usually because in early life as children they felt rejected, excluded or hated by others, unlovable in some way and have suffered degrading experiences that ate like acid into their being, so they keep a defense, they pretend not to care at all. In adult years they often are more autonomous and solitary in their lives than others, seeming not to need anyone, or pretending not to. Even though they form relationships, there is a part of the self that is withheld. The fear of rejection goes so deep in some, that they reject others first, or psychologically refuse to move forwards from friendship, from casual acquaintance or some other " safe" stage in the relationship.

If you have a retrograde Venus in your chart, the first step to releasing yourself from the lonely prison you have created in love is to recognize how Venus is acting in your particular chart. Why are you turned away from love, why are you turned inside yourself ? The answer is in your chart somewhere. More can be told about the individual life history and problem, from the house and sign of Venus and her aspects to other planets, her rulerships. The second step is to make a conscious effort to be more open to people, more open to love. To value yourself by realizing the rejections and hate leveled at you were in the past, not the present, there is no need to perpetuate them. No need to continue to believe the lies people told you about yourself that you were unlovable, unattractive, not worth respecting. You know these are lies. Begin to be the person you are now, Leave the scars of the past to the past. Others will love you for who you are now. Retrograde planets cause problems by perpetuating the past, but psychologically it is our own mind that allows the past to persist, and we have the power to alter that. To turn our Venus and our life around, to meet our true soul mate.

If you have a retrograde Venus in your chart, you will be happiest if you seek a partner who has a retrogrde Mars.

Foreign Affairs.

People who have formed a deep spiritual, mental or physical bond in a past life cannot be ever be separated. Not by distance, not by time, not by class or race or any barrier. Such souls will always have a destiny to meet. A fated path that impels them irresistibly towards each other, even from across the other side of the world. Until they meet and recognize each other they do not even know they walk that path towards each other. Is your soul mate from a far off land?.

Astrological clues to whether your soul mate could be from a foreign land

The ruler of the seventh house, in the ninth house. The ninth house rules far flung places, and the seventh love, marriage and soul mates. So this is one simple testimony that there is a possibility your soul mate could hail from a far off land. But the first rule of astrology is that we never judge a chart on one aspect alone. What we look for are several corroborating aspects, that tell the same tale. The more aspects that point to an over seas romance or a long distance lover, that more likely the soul mate will be an interesting foreigner.

If there is only this one signpost pointing to a foreign land in the chart, it is a mere possibility; it is just as likely that the soul mate would be connected with other ninth house activities, for example, university, a library, a church or temple, ones religion., ones political involvements. An experienced astrologer will be able to use his intuition, and his knowledge of the client to make a correct judgment, in a such a case, an amateur needs to meticulously follow all the rules without deviation, until he has sufficient experience to make any judgment on just one feature of the chart..

Here are a few other signs and clues:

Neptune, planet of travel, closely aspecting the seventh house.

The ruler of the seventh house conjunct Neptune.

Ruler of the ninth house in the seventh.

The ruler of the seventh house conjunct Jupiter; these aspects become strengthened if the ruler of the seventh house also falls in the ninth house

Jupiter in the eighth house, traditionally means a foreign lover. Neptune in the eighth a foreign lover or a dreamy romantic sex life.

Chiron in the ninth house aspecting the seventh cusp.

If Venus and the ruler of the seventh house are both Cadent.

In a male chart the Moon in the ninth.

Uranus in seventh house. This aspect means a soul mate from a very different background. It doesn't always mean foreigner, but when other indications of a far off love are in the chart it might do.

Usually to be certain the aspects must tie up in a much more complex way, these simple signs, show only a possibility. The working astrologer needs to assess his clients life and attitudes very carefully from her chart before jumping to conclusion that his client will marry and emigrate. The aspects can be misleading in some cases.

An astrologer must use, judgment, intuition and common sense. Some people live lives where they barely cross the threshold of their back door. Others use planes as casually as calling a taxi, or walking down the street and travel is an intrinsic part of their daily life. The chart always reflects the clients life, but even the more meticulous and methodical astrologers are prone to misinterpret occasionally. If we know our client has a sheltered traditional life, has never left her remote Indian village and is never likely to, and that her marriage will be an arranged one. Influenced by family, cast, and money. That she has no relatives abroad, then, it is more likely that aspects to do with far distances and foreign places, means a place which the client will consider far away", even if that place is just a few hundred miles down the road from her own village. Individuals live individual life's, in astrology we attempt to make one rule fit all information, which it never does.

To predict a lover from another continent and emigration, would seem shattering, unlikely and possibly not even relevant to such a clients. The personal knowledge you hold about your client, may help to make a more accurate judgment, if the chart is not totally clear, but equally personal knowledge can sometimes mislead. There is after all the outside chance that our local village girl, will indeed fall in love with a foreign explorer and be able to defy all local convention to marry him. So we must use such information cautiously and work only with the charts own aspects. If one size doesn't fit all, or one rule doesn't apply to all, we may as well throw away the rule book you might say. This is why I teach you in my own particular and special way. I teach you to look, to think, to analyze and reason, not to copy a list of statements and imagine they will do for every chart. Astrology is always about individuality.

In fifty or a hundred years. The pages of histories have turned. Internet, modern means of travel and world economies, migrant workers, have all change the face of how we meet live and work, mix with people. It has made the astrologers task more difficult and far more interesting. A hundred years ago an astrologer had only local clients, and would hardly ever be asked about love in far off climes. Research is still a little slow. In a case like the example of the Indian girl, in her remote mountain village the astrologer must try and judge, whether the Neptune and others aspect he has perceived do indeed mean an over seas lover, or simply someone from a city further away.

If our client is from the United States, does another country that seems to be shown in her chart simply mean another state? These are questions to be asked. The beginner must content himself to use words like " far away", and " Not a local person". The more experience astrologer must strive to be precise so he can tell the person not only if their soul mate is a foreigner, or a local man, but where exactly in the world he or she is from.

Not Foreign Enough

How aspects can be deceptive for the beginner

I recall in my own early days of inexperience, A beginner at astrology, I had done a soul mate reading for an elderly English lady. Her name was Emma, but she'd always been called Emerald. Venus was retrograde at the ninth house cusp in Scorpio. House of overseas places. Neptune was in the seventh in Virgo. Virgo's ruler was in the ninth house. Her chart had some of the distinctive hall marks of one who would marry a man from a foreign land. I described his physical appearance in detail as best I could. He is a stranger from abroad. I added

It was told later that the chart reading made her shudder. long ago she had developed an unease and antipathy to all foreign men. Never ventured abroad. Never wanted to. Nothing would induce her to marry a foreigner now, she said. The chart echoed something in her life she said , but she hoped it was passed. He story emerged. As a young women wanting independence from her strict authoritarian home she had lived and worked opposite a dockside. A rough port of dark streets, where few women ever went. Those who did were usually prostitutes. late one night, returning home she had been frightened by a drunken Danish sailor. A small incident, but because of her sheltered genteel background and her inexperience and feelings of vulnerability at the time, it made an unduly deep impression. So much that she became afraid to go out at night. He had jumped out at her in the dark, in a high spirited staggering clumsy groping grabbing loud voiced way, wouldn't let her pass without a kiss. The men nearby on the dock had not come to her rescue. She didn't speak their language but interpreted their shouts as jeering as goading him on. It unnerved her, more than she liked to admit. She looked for another job, another flat. She'd never felt safe afterwards surrounded by men, less so by foreigners.

There had been very few men in Emma's life. As we might suppose from her seventh house Neptune, there had been platonic and unrequited loves. Fastidious and finicky, Emma said of herself she was " A spinster , an old maid in the making" Then later in life a Jamaican lover had robbed her of money in a cruel confidence trick and broke her heart. She had learned her lesson she said. Emerald disliked and mistrusted foreign men of all descriptions. She had no interest in travel, learning languages, or foreigner lands despite her ninth house Venus, and would not have felt secure outside England.

She came from a narrow kind of background, where in her youth marriage to a foreigner, especially a dark skinned man like her Jamaican lover would have created immense prejudices and disapproval, "I'd have been written off, disowned without a penny to my name. It just wasn't done. " she said " Unless he'd happened to be an Indian Prince or something Then it would have been ok! Money always makes things right. That is what it was like in those days, all petty prejudices, there wasn't the liberation have now. No tolerance, no humanity, no real love. Thank God that I didn't get pregnant. That would have been the pits as far as my family were concerned!." she said. "He was an ordinary working man, not a Prince. A rogue and a charmer. Beautiful, Affectionate, kind, a wonderful lover. Warm enough to melt my old spinsterish soul," Emerald quaintly put it. "I had to keep the loss of money secret and survive on nothing for fear my indiscretion came out. It utterly devastated my life. It took years to recoup financially, to get back to where I was, and emotionally I don't think I ever did"

Emerald was much more modern, progressive and open-minded than the background she sprang from but she'd still carried her past like a guilty secret that stained her reputation, instead of the mistaken foolish but wonderful love affair it was. Long after her parents passed away some of this same old ingraining and concern for reputation, for how things looked. lived on in her own character. One could still see the refinement and genteel spinster in her manner and ways. Her neat dress, barely any make up. Her healthy outdoor Sagittarian looks, her quick striding athletic step. (mars sun Sagittarius). Her nimble mercurial movements. Her shy discreet twelfth house moon. that gave its air of Aquarian detachment and made her more progressive, in secret, than her background and family intended her to be. The story is in the chart for you to read. All charts are biographies in symbolic form.

Chart for Emerald

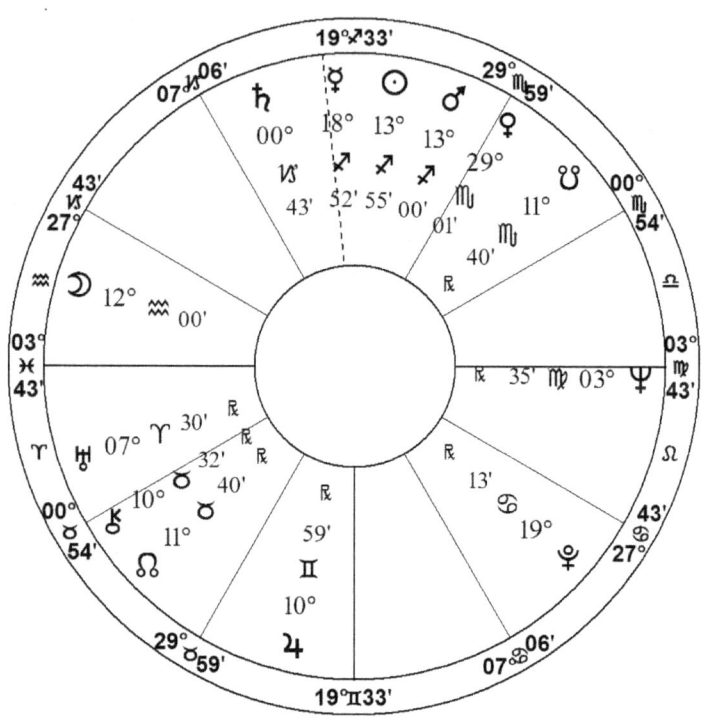

With Neptune in her seventh house, (which presumably had been badly aspected by a transit on the night she encountered the Dane) and a ninth house Venus. Two testimonies towards a lover from a far off place and knowing nothing of her background or preferences. I had described to her a foreign man with dark Italian looks, a wave or curl in his hair, a thin, a neat dresser. (Virgo, Neptune). Suffers a little with his nerves, dyspepsia, psychosomatic, owned a premier cat and liked classical music. I ended by saying He is not English, a true foreigner..

At the time of the consultation she was dismayed. A year later she met the man described and became involved with him rather quickly. She told me everything I said was correct, his initials, his looks, his craggy face, his background of drifting in and out of business ventures, and typical of her retrograde Venus this love had come late in life. But he was not foreign, to quote Emerald " He is more English than cricket" and had no foreign connections that she could find at all. He did not even hail from the next town, and had no foreign ancestry. She had asked me if this could possibly be her soul mate? For in the depth of her being she felt and hoped he was.

On examining both charts I was reassured that he was indeed her soul mate, no two charts were better matched. But being less experience in those days, I was puzzled and disturbed over the way I had misread the very clear travel or foreign aspects that appeared in the chart. How had these manifested? What had I missed? Do you know the answer dear reader? Perhaps you do, think on it. Aspects are impelled always come out in some way, even when they work in a way we don't expect. Astrologers are human they are not infallible, but when an Astrologer finds a contradiction, a discrepancy between what he predicts and what happens, or if he cannot see an important facet of a situation in advance, he must back track over his work and use hindsight to find where he was wrong so that he learns for next time. I asked Emerald if she would help me find the error of my methods and ways and tell me more about this love.

On further correspondence, she revealed that she'd found him at "Meeting" at the local spiritualist church. A church where people go to communicate with the dead; This will sound macabre to some readers. Spiritualist churches are common in England and the USA, but less familiar in other countries. The services are called "meetings" usually a hymn is sung and a person known as the Medium, who is a kind of intermediary between the living souls and their dead relatives, brings messages from the dead. This kind of unorthodox church would certainly have been disapproved of by Emerald's strict background. but in her long life she'd overcome many impairments of her upbringing.

In her chart ninth house Venus, is close to the cusp between the eighth and ninth. The sign of Scorpio, Venus sign occupying the eighth house, house of death and reincarnation, as well as the ninth. This being retrograde it is also an inturned Venus, Venus turned inside to itself, to the past, or in this case turned inwards to the spiritual world, not turned outside to the outer world.

When she was in her early sixties she accompanied a female friend there. The friend was a 'game for anything' type, she did not believe in sprits, but thought it would be " entertaining." (Pisces rising, an openness to spirituality in various forms. Neptune opposite and ruling over the ascendant, the dissolving of past prejudges). The church, its doctrines, regular meetings and "Spirit" had since then become gradually a more important part of Emerald's life. Her new adopted religion. The soul mate with the dark Italian looks came into her life a year later. He was a visiting spiritualist medium at her church. He was English born, highly educated like Emma, his accent was cultured, more so than the locals. Semi retired, but still involved himself in various business schemes. A good orator, who led the prayer meetings, sermons and songs. A communicator with dead souls (Neptune, psychic powers). One who tries to bring proof of an afterlife by attuning, through his "spirit guide", to the dead and giving messages in words to their living family.

This story illustrates how easy it can be to misinterpret a chart. knowledge of the clients background, her prejudice against foreigners, her new found interest in spiritualism, would have helped in this case. But regardless of any prior knowledge the picture was embedded in her chart, it was there to be seen, being inexperienced I did not look at it closely enough, my assumption were mistakes and commonplace. I did not look for less obvious or more complex possibilities, consequently I did not see the whole picture. Always weigh up the rulers aspects, and look at the whole chart, if you have serious doubts then ask the client for information if necessary, and use common sense before jumping to conclusions that may be incorrect. Usually the more complex the person, the more complex the interpretation of the chart can be.

Remember in astrology an aspect always *has* to manifest. It is like a river flowing into the future, it cannot stop. If one direction is blocked, (as in this ladies life, a capacity for all things foreign was blocked by her unfortunate experience at the docks, her financial loss in overseas business, her strict close knit background, and her own fears and prejudges,) it will manifest in the next way it can, or next esoteric level. like a river flooding over the land next to the blockage and creating a new stream. In the client charts, the psychic world, was the next esoteric level, it was unknown territory, a foreign land of the mind, that is remote inaccessible and foreign to her, since she was not spiritualist herself, And her soul mate came out of there, out of that mysterious spirit land if you like. Judging which level an event or situation is going to manifest, is not always straight forwards. Even love itself has these levels, a soul mate love is usually holistic but sometimes love remains in the mental metaphysic sphere, in say unrequited love and it cannot quite materialize down to the next level, that of the every day world

Something blocked at the material physical or every day level often gets pushed in to the mental or spiritual level. The alternative level would have been education, another ninth house matter, but our Lady studied at an elite and private girls school; Then at a lady's college, Boys and men were excluded. The labyrinth of education and universities was not an alien unknown foreign land to her. Her chart in all its aspects stresses the unknown. So it manifested on a spiritual level the spiritual aspect, the church building, the meeting, the friend who took her there, came to the fore when all other avenues through which the aspect might have operated blocked love out. Through the church, a ninth house building, it materialized in her life in a solid way. The travel to unknown countries instead of coming to the fore in a direct way in her destiny remained in the background, in a non material way, in the mental journey into the foreign territory of the new church and its beliefs..

Twin Soul.

Referring to the metaphysical structure of life in the first part of the book, Volume One. I gave a list of popular definition of Soul Mates. There is also the term "spiritual twin", and clients have wondered if a twin soul is always a twin spirit? Yes, a *true* twin soul is always a Twin spirit too.

Some people believe that when our soul and spirit was created, before time began, and before we walked the earth, the essence or substance of our soul and spirit was split into two, like identical twins in the mothers womb, but our womb was time and space and whatever existed between worlds. A twin soul is the same as us on a very deep level but also uniquely different. If we meet a twin soul it is a rare relationship. And it isn't always a romantic one, though it can be. A twin soul can be a person of either sex, any age, it can even be a figure from history, or someone we have never met, but who we seem to have so much in common with we instinctively feel we are them, or were them in another life, or that we should have known them, as friend or lover. When twin souls meet up, regardless of whether they are best friend, or lovers, business partners, or family members, they are usually inseparable. A bond that may last a life time, even if it not continual and has long gaps between meetings. The relationship on the human level can be quite different in each case, depending on the age and sex of the twin, and what power or purposes of fate has brought them into our life.

A Soul mate, can be a twin soul too, hence there is much confusion in the terms, but it isn't always!. A soul mate does not have to be a twin soul. The relationship between soul mates is always romantic, a love relationship, between people. Usually one that has covered many lives, many past incarnations, which is why the love between them feels more magical and intense. And any other emotions it arouses feel more intense too, like jealousies for example. Soul mates are not always made from our same essence at the dawn of time, but rather they are another human soul with its own essence, but one that will complete us, on the earthly level. like an exact match, a soul mate has what we need to complete us and help us evolve as a spirit, and we have what he needs.

If you think of our human essence, as being like a Russian doll where one doll is hidden inside the other, There are many layers of mind and spirit and soul within that essence, one wrapped inside the other. The soul is a deeper layer, of us; Then the spirit. Then the mind, Then body. The links between souls are deeper than those between spirits, the soul link goes back to its very core of existences. But when the souls essence is split into two (or more), the spirits essence the next layer down in the Russian doll is automatically divided too. If it didn't, you'd get a unique situation where two people, two souls, shared a spirit, and total telepathy. There are legends about such people or races. They may exist, but very rarely, just as on the physical level you get Siamese twins who exist, but rarely. If the spirits essence doesn't divide fully, which is more common place, you get fragments of telepathy and knowing between the twin souls, and soul mates but never total.

A twin soul is always a twin spirit, because the essence is shared. So the terms are used interchangeably.

But, now there is a complication in definition, a twin spirit, doesn't *have* to be a twin soul. A twin spirit can simply be someone whose spirit is made in a similar pattern, like two rare birds, who are not related or connected at essence but are somehow of the same make, and have gravitated together because of that similarity. When an encounter occurs there is an affinity, a recognition. These two know they are alike in a world where all others seem different. In modern science it is said that the chances of two unknown and unrelated people having the same DNA is very remote but not impossible. This is the same. It is rare but can happen.

Let us come down to another layer in our doll. A Spiritual twin; Someone who is not necessarily our own soul essence, but someone very like us in spirit. The term again. Like "twin spirit", is often used in a casual lighter less deep way, to describe someone we have a lot in common with. That is to say their spirit is like ours, or even linked to ours in some mysterious way, but their soul or deeper essence that goes back to creation is not. Spiritual twins are more common. A twin spirit, once we have met one; is usually is more precious to us than the spiritual twins we may meet along the way, (because a twin spirit may have the same essence, or even if it hasn't it has often has more in common in all its ethereal layers).

With a spiritual twin the relationship is often less close or intense, and describes a relationship that is purely spiritual, or intellectual, a relationship the mind, and character, or based around the same artistic talent and appreciations, or same faith, it doesn't always transgress the boundaries into romantic, or sexual love. Though humans being human it sometimes does! Especially when the twin is of appropriate age and gender and physically attractive. But whatever the relationship is composed of, and it is often work, there is always an affinity, with a spiritual twin. Spiritual twins always share something, say the same beliefs, motivation or studies, or same aims or task in life. They are like two friends with a common purpose. Two disciples who share a common faith or art. But they tend to have quite separate lives too. A term used in a lighter less deep sense, to describe someone we have a lot in common with intellectually or mentally.

The nomenclature is always confusing because, not only do these states of being sometime overlap, like a twin soul also being a town spirit, but also people so often use these two terms in a casual way, rather than a technically correct way, to mean the same thing. In love it is the experience that counts not the definition of it

A persons chart is always a unique history When you are living through that era of your private history you are not necessarily going to know if it's a soul mate you have met or a spirit twin, for if you have only experience of one, you have nothing to compare it with to define it or differentiate it, you simply have to live it and see where it leads.

Soul Mates, and twins are linked by a psychic bond, that transcends time and the present life, though neither are usually aware of that bond, except that it tugs the heart, it brings intense and often mystifying love for a person one hardly knows anything about. Astrology can help decide if it's a soul mate, or a spirit twin or something else, if someone is your soul mate you may be afraid of loosing him, if you have lost someone already but find he wasn't the true soul mate, there can be a modicum of comfort in knowing that one day the true soul mate will come. But at the end of the day, you are still feeling what you feel for the person and have to finish that inner journey of a love and grief and pain in its own time,. You cannot always alter your feelings. Definitions make the picture a little clearer that's all. But the importance is not is not in the definition, but in the living experience of every day love.

Metaphysical layers

If you visualize a human as our Russian Doll, one level within the other. Just a as the astrology chart has one level that can be unwound within another in the same chart. From the physical material body to immortal soul that is beyond time. The layers become increasingly finer, higher or more evolved in substance. There is an interchange between them, for we live through all the components of our being, not just one. They go like this.

The physical or earthly material Body.

Two people joined on this level are biological twins, who may be identical or non identical. They are not necessarily twins in any other spiritual way, though they can be. Biological twin have unusual experiences.

The Etheric or ethereal.

Our twins and connections on the etheric levels are firstly our own " astral body" The etheric is the vibrations or magnetic field between the atoms of matter. Fate twins, people who seem to live out similar live and fate though are in no way connected and may even be from other times. They are attuned to the same sort of spiritual vibration, but not necessarily alike. Some may be the same soul race or soul family as us, but not securely.

The Mind. Our mental and spiritual twins come from this level are "the like mined people", in various degrees, these include spiritual twins. In the astrology chart this is the level of the interior, events that happen to our inner being. Like a parting from someone which can be physical since the person goes physically out of life and sight, but which effects us more emotionally.

The chart like our being works through layers of existence, if it cannot work one way it works another.

Saturn in the astrology chart, will work through the physical realm by brining a dark cloudy day, in the ethereal level the same aspect may give a heavy atmosphere felt only by the senses as a darkness. On the mental level, he be depression, on the instinctive level an awareness of impending doom of some kind.

The mind can be further divided into all its layers, like the Russian doll, the emotion, sometimes called the" emotional body" or the Heart, for it has to do with feeling sensations emotionally rather than physically. The emotional body gives us an empathy with people and situations that are not our own. We are linked to them in the way that all humanity is linked. The instinctive mind, which is the seat of our instincts, and superstition on this level we connected with Totem animals and archetypes., with the path of luck good and bad. In the astrology chart this is the equality of living through the negative or positive side of a planet or aspect.

The logical mind, is another doll, and is the more scientific and evolved of our minds layers. After the mind on another remoter more esoteric octave comes Spirit. The spirit is higher than the mind Through spirit we are aware of mind, and the other levels and how they integrate together in our life. On the spirit level we meet our Twin spirits.

The Soul. The Soul being the innermost or higher most bond between beings. Twin souls, Soul mates, and soul bonds. Are formed on this level from the same essence as us. The soul also connected with our karma

We should not trouble to much about which term is correct or incorrect. It would make for considerable clarity if everyone used the same definition, but it is human nature not to. The sum total is always more than it the parts anyway. A twin spirit is never just a twin spirits it is more, a soul Mate is never just a soul mate it transcends definitions, it is an experience more than we can express or even have words for.

Mis-directions

In the first part of the book we looked at infatuations, and the Animus effect. How it can misdirect the mind from real love and leave us to walk in the wilderness of loneliness and pain. In this book let us explore the past and how it can sometime mislead the person in search of a soul mate. I this volume we look at the Path of remembrance and then the sexual labyrinth.

The Ghost Of The Past

When you loss someone dear to you at a critical time. There is an absence in the soul, where that person used to be. There is also emotions, unusually to do with abandonment, and being powerless to change anything, These are the emotions we shut away in prisons inside our self, along with everything else that we can not face at the time. We are too busy dealing with the immediate events, the ending of the relationship, or grief, Anger, loss, the prospect of the long term influences of adverse change amour life. We are coping with the every day things. The loss can be in childhood it can be death of parent, A parting with a dear friend, moving away. But always an ending, something stops. While life goes on, and all we have locked up in the prison inside our dark mind from that time. The feelings, the images, the sounds, the smells, every little detail remains locked. Like a box of forgotten memories and souvenirs.

So time moves on. The amount of time depends on the cycle of the planet.

An obsessive love, isn't always an anima projection. It can be the result of a distorted distant memory. Someone you desperately wanted to remain in your life, but were powerless to hold onto. An example is a child whose father died, the child can do nothing at all Love is hacked away. The years go on. Life goes on. Then some detail transports us back, a smell, a sound, a certain look in a person's eyes, it strikes direct into the raw pain of memory, except we cannot remember the connection, only the subconscious does. The new obsessive love reminds us in some subtle way of the other person, the one we lost long ago.

The subconscious recognizes the resemblance, but our conscious mind never does. (if it did, no obsession would ensue), To the subconscious it is almost as if we'd been given a second chance, to have this person back, and to hang onto him or her, to change the fate of years ago. So the spirit is desperate to hang onto it. There follows a kind of infatuation. The key to becoming free of such an infatuation is to remember, who it is, the love reminds you of and why. This is far more difficult than it sounds.

The way in which the person resembles the past one like a mask, so obscure so subtle, so distorted and beyond memory that first efforts at memory are unlikely to bring any response. Only the subconscious has the answer.

If the conscious mind recognized the memory, the past would not have such a ferocious hold. Usually the resemblance it has little to do with looks, but often a great deal to do with loss. You have to analyze the whole situation. Once the mind has that vital piece of the past correct in its place it can move on. The infatuation will fall away and relinquish its power to imprison you. In one case it was it was as subtle as background music. This is Helga's chart and story. She met a man in a place where the band was playing a certain piece of music. She did not connect the music to her life, it didn't evoke any memories, but her mood was sad. It was late afternoon, she sat in a pavement cafe in the cathedral square and sipped coffee, stirred with sugar on a stick.

Some sixteen or seventeen years before meeting the man; this lady had been a student in her mid twenties and transit Saturn, her ruling planet, had been crossing the ascendant to conjunct with Pluto.

Chart for Helga

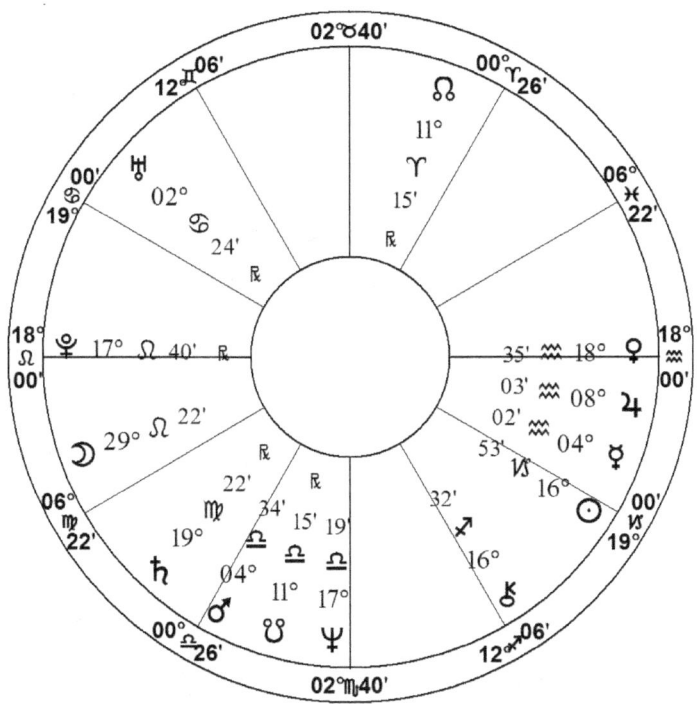

She had tea and iced ginger cake with her favorite aunt in a different hotel in a different place in East Germany. Then on a winter's afternoon under a few falling snow flakes she parted with her Aunt forever. The client, Helga, boarded a tram and returned to her university; The aunt next day set off from her hotel to join her new husband and was involved in a fatal car crash. The same music, the same the same winter chill in the air, same mood, even some of the same clothes fashions had come around. She met a traveler. A man who bore no resemble to her aunt, except that he came and sat at her table. And while her mind registered something "familiar " that she couldn't grasp, he chatted about the long car journey he had ahead of him to meet with his fiancé that icy afternoon, and she felt desperately and hopelessly that she loved him and that now she had met him, she could not let him go. Superficially he was handsome and appealed to her. The compulsive tie cannot exist without that, the surface attraction too, it helps misdirect and mask and obscure the deeper memory. But it was the underlying attraction that bound her so tightly and painfully to this doomed relationship. Just as the relationship with her aunt was doomed to death. So this relationship was doomed to end or to never begin because of his fiancé. Her subconscious even responded to the sense of doom. The mind plays strange tricks.

Looking at the astrological analysis of Helga's chart; the Venus-Pluto opposition shows a life transfigured by love. Pluto is ruler of her fourth house, family, Helga's young aunt whom she loved dearly. Pluto can also be trauma, shock, sudden endings. The story of her aunt is written here. Pluto's aspect to third house Neptune, a dangerous journey resulting in sudden death. Neptune is the ruler of Helga's house of death

It might have ended at that but Pluto is retrograde. So when the man came into her into her life, Helga thinks it was 1993 or 94. Transit Saturn would be in the reverse position, stirring everything up again, including memories that remained subconscious, Pluto rules the subconscious. The subtle things like the music, the time of year, the smell of the coffee, everything just exactly the same. It is the culmination of small things, not one small thing, you smell coffee a million times, but one day it's the same coffee, same smell mingled with the same sounds. Transit Saturn was conjunct Venus, Pluto is the aunt, Venus is love, this new conjunction a new love. It is on her seventh house opposing Pluto this time. But re activating Pluto, making feelings surface, this man desperation, that if she lets this stranger go, she will never see him again. The midpoints on this chart add a touch of hopelessness. Neptune is trine to Venus, showing a proclivity to love at first sight. Also to be hurt by love at first sight since Chiron is midpoint between Neptune and Venus, and in the fifth house. Even without Pluto aspecting all three planets, there is tragedy and deep feelings here.,

Chiron symbolizes hurt but he also represents healing. At first Helga watched the man walk out of her life. We do not have his chart, but we don't need it because it would not have fitted with hers anyway. Hindsight was to prove that. That afternoon she only felt the pain of a hopeless love, she felt she was dying, she felt she was mad. She could not understand how she could be so gripped by a stranger. She was married, not unhappy, the man was so much younger. Nothing fitted. She haunted the place she met him, in the vain hope of meeting him again. and it was only inch by inch the memories came back, the music associated with her aunt. Music is a Neptune thing too. Coffee or Tea and cakes are quite a Venus thing. The great sorrow of parting that she would never see her aunt again. Because Helga managed to find this displacement she could put her emotions in their right place. The grief for her aunt, the love, the passing affinity with the young man, who, like her aunt all those years ago, shared her table and was going happily to his future.

To return to our subject; when it feels like a soul mate has touched our life with his, but turns out to be an anima projection, or as in Helga's case, a displacement from the past, there are certain things to look for in the charts, they show more clearly in synastry if the charts of both people are available.

Astrological Clues

In the Synastry between the two charts, there will be no soul mate connections. In Anima relationships as we said it is often Neptune - Moon, or Pluto Venus connections. In displacement from the past. Neptune can be involved, since he is the planet of illusions and reflections, it is often Saturn – Venus connection are often involved, usually. Twelfth house connections. Sometimes, sun Saturn or ruler of the eighth houses are connected in the twelfth house. The twelfth house is the House of subconscious memory.

In each subsequent volume we will explore a different path in the maze of confusion. To meet your true soul mate you must avoid the wrong paths, or if you cannot, you must find your way out before you become lost to the treachery of loves illusion. This is one way of find the right path. Through these studies you will also learn the psychology of love. We could put it in one volume, but it easier to eat in small bites and much more interesting, a few drops of rain will water a plant and its leaves will reach to the sun,, a deluge will drown it. So to avoid mental overload the lessons in, each of my books are variety of short pieces.

Of Unrequited Love.

Most people hope to meet and spend eternity with their love. But there can be many obstacles to that simple hope. The person may be already married, They may not love us in return., or they may love us but not enough to make the future work. We cannot always claim the person we love. Love is always deep but destiny is deeper and sometimes chooses otherwise. When that happens we have to go on alone, to repair our broken dreams, rebuild our life but differently and make the best of what is left to us. We have to remember that time does heal and time does move on, and even when the world seems at its most bleak, a new love can arrive that is greater than the old and can transform our life in a second.

Never despair, never give up. Sometimes fate brings us someone who is out of reach. Sometime we think we will never find even one love in a whole life time. To expect too much is as foolish as to accept too little. Life is awash with possibilities and life is always changing. Take strength from the fact that noting stays the same, and so there is always the prospect of something better..

I will now illustrate, a not unusual episode of unrequited love, with my client Beth. Her story is common place but best told in her own words in an extract from her letters to me.

CASE HISTORY

"Four years ago I was sure I had met my soul mate. How else could you love someone from a far for so long and stay in a job you hated, just to see him every day, when its painful for you. Now he's relocating and in effect leaving me. For four years there has been looks between us and nothing else. It has been hell for me these past four years. But now fate has stepped in. When the company of which he is a director moves to bigger premises it will be too far for me to travel."

The question: What was it about this chart that predisposed Beth to experience such a long and painful interlude in her life ?. There are at least five things, but the more you study the chart the more you will find.

1, The ruler of her house of soul mates, Venus, is in Trine with Neptune. Neptune is the capacity to delude oneself, and Venus about love. Such an aspect would not always mean unhappy or unrealistic love but it is an aspect that makes us beware of the possibly, and look for further indications.

2, Neptune forms the Venus trine from the house of sorrows and difficulties, (twelfth house) suggesting a negative interpretation., rather than a positive one.

Neptune could have indicated a long distance love, not securely a one sided love. But we know Beth and her boss are in the same work place. It is interesting that we also know from her letter that it is long distance that will bring the relationship or illusion to its end. Neptune interpreted negatively is about illusions and Venus is about love. The twelfth house is about sorrows.

Chart For Beth

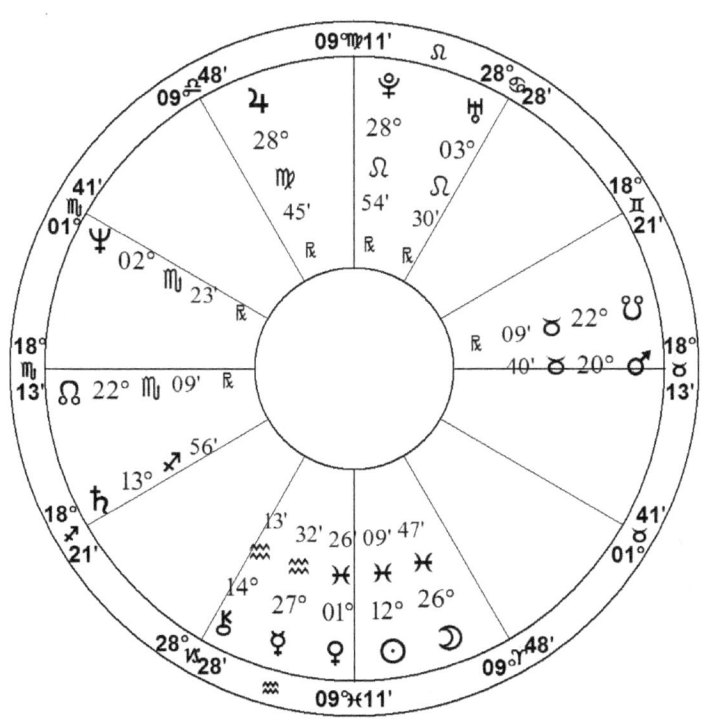

3, Venus is on the cusp of a sign, cuspal planets tend to act in a worse way than when they are non cuspal . This one means difficult emotional changes. Because Venus is fractionally more into a water sign.

4 Venus forms a quincunx to Uranus; While Neptune forms a square to Uranus. Since Venus and Neptune form a trine to each other, these aspects are knotted together, like one complex tangled aspect. A Quincunx is a severe and damaging stress aspect, something that pulls the mind or tears the fabric of your life apart. The square too is a hard aspect. Uranus is something that suddenly befalls you, a situation which is unsought, and unjust. It happens due to fate or circumstance, and ends equally as suddenly as it starts. In Beth's chart Uranus being in the ninth, house of distances and travel, and Uranus circumstance beyond her own control or making, we again see the vivid picture of its ending. This aspect suggest the episode may also bring Beth close to a nervous break down or mental illness, Nothing Beth says is over stated; the reverse, when she speaks of pain she means torment, agony, when she speaks of hell, it is accurate. This combination of aspects is like a fracture running through the chart.

4 Pluto opposes Venus, Pluto is obsession, Venus is love. This opposition is not exact, since Pluto is in 29th degree of Leo and Venus in the first of Pisces, rather than the last degree of Virgo, but it has influence. Pluto describes Beth's boss, a figure of power, (She once described him to me as having eyes like coals, black and, shiny, contrasting starkly with his dark gold spiky hair. Broad shoulder, slim hips and always

immaculately tidy. This fits so well with Pluto in Virgo.)

5 The south node conjuncts Mars over the cusp of the house of soul mates. The south node is what pulls back to the past, it can be past karma or the present life, an inability to move forwards, and away, the node drags backwards. If Venus is love than Mars is passion, this aspects shows that she is powerless to leave it behind, she is always dragged back into the obsession, This aspect alone would not predispose her to unrequited love, especial not in an earth sign, but because of all the other unrequited aspects it makes it difficult for her to let go.

"I find it hard to leave him even though there is nothing between us"

6. Saturn 'afflicts' the house of soul mate. He forms a quincunx to that house, and also to Mars who occupies the house. Saturn tends to be things which endure, an enduring, or long standing stressful situation. Saturn is tied loosely into to the love knot of aspects, because he is also in square to the Pisces sun. Bringing us back to Neptune, Pisces ruler.

7. You cannot know this but, I add it for good measure. In the past Beth asked for a Synastry she wrote.

"I sense he feels something. Being the director and married with a family would make it hard for him to show any feelings for me I suppose " At that time she was desperate but not ready to give up her delusion, not strong enough, to acknowledge that it was all a one sided dream. She hoped the Synastry would confirm he also felt this way. It did not. There are no strong Synastry aspects between the two charts. So I have not included the chart. No real connections between two charts mean no real connections between the two lives.

This is further testimony to an unrequited or one side love without hope. This illustration is not meant to provide solution, it is only to help you assess a chart to detect if the love is realistic, if it can become mutual, or if you are dealing with love without hope. But to conclude this case history on a brighter note. Our mind already knows, what the chart echoes and subconsciously it works through this in its own time. We can guide the person, but we cannot push them, we cannot make the blind see. Her last letter implies she had faced her lowest point, and gone past it, it foreshadows a progress that she isn't yet aware of. She wrote

"I leave at the end of the month, fate has played a cruel joke on me. Anyway if there is any light to be shed on my situation, could you please advise me"

Beth's willingness to acknowledge that the love must end and that it really is un required is the first step towards her recovery. She has left hope behind and found acceptance and is now seeking explanations, seeking help to make sense of it all. she is no longer clinging to a delusion she has begun to walk away emotionally, but she walks on thin ice, she is still wounded, bewildered and fragile mentally

Dear reader, if you have purchased the first book in the soul mate series, you may like to refer back to that Soul mate book under the section about anima projection and infatuation. As to how it works and how to free oneself.

To add a final note. Why should this happen now?, Beth's unhappy romance began in the year 2000. I don't know the exact month or day; The love knot of aspects, as I have termed it lying dormant like a wreath in her chart appears to have been triggered when transit Neptune, opposed Radix Uranus.

It began to end and Beth began to emerge from the dream towards the end of 2004, (Transit Uranus having crossed radix Venus, and begun moving out of orb from radix Neptune) the clients last letter was dated January 2005.

The Sexual Labyrinth

It is easy to be lead astray on the road of love. If you desire to find your true soul mate and ultimate happiness, but you only seem to stumble on disappointing or tormenting relationship, you must eliminate each wrong path. Every time you terminate a wrong direction, you come closer to the right one. Eventually there is only one path you can go. In this series of books, we look at paths of misdirects, wrong roads you may take and become lost in.

Sexual attraction is a very common path to loss ones way on. Too often the lure of sexual desire is both so subtle we do not recognize it and so overpowering we cannot avoid it. Sex and its sensations, its cravings and evocative dreams of half promised but unspoken futures, it temporary satisfaction, and the way it can make the hunger and loneliness stop for a time are mistaken for love. For some people sex and love cannot be separated in the emotions, or untangled in the heady mental confusion of romance are always mingled The nature of both sex and love lie in an ecstasy between two worlds. When the first misting of the senses vanishes like the mist on the shore. There can be little left to hold the couple together, if sex was all there was in the beginning. To the person in the relationship, love will seem to change, but all it is that the curtain of desires illusion is fading and the daylight is showing through the dream. The thread bare reality of a relationship with someone whom there is little sympathy and little in common begins to creep out of the cobwebs. Nothing has changed but the dream.

A good sexual relationship can reveal to you the true nature of your desires. But there is a difference between the ecstatic merging of souls and the quenching of the embers of passion in sex. The former can last for a life time. With soul mates there is an empathy of common interests, attitudes, shared goals. and it is likely that the harmony in love and marriage between two people will be lasting. Where the persons are drawn together only through the illusion of sensuality and external matters of attraction. Like wealth or good looks, which can be just as alluring;

The relationship is sort of relationship one can dream about but find no substance behind it eventually, because the attraction is based on illusion and the lure of sex, it will not be happy or last., the first dazzling spell of love will be followed by a the winter of a colder less happy relationship, that deteriorates, develops many faults and only seems mended or patched up in each others arms, the cracks of the relationship are papered over temporarily, soon to fall apart again. For two such souls have nothing else to give each other., Sex is fine and noble, it is part of the framework of a relationship. A wonderful pastime, but it's a mistake to build your whole life or all your hopes around it.

At times it will be sensed when there is nothing there of worth but sex, like a impression of winter, the cold ending of the relationship as it drifts further through time. But in many cases only one of the lovers will know of the impeding separation. Like two horses temporary shackled together one will feel bound to the other for life, the other will know it will one day it will pull free of the yoke, and move on alone looking for something new. This is the scenario of many mismatched relationships. But how do you tell if its only sex, when it feels like love?

Astrologically, There will be no soul mate aspects linking the two charts. Very few other aspects. If your charts have little in common, it is likely you and he will have little in common. But there will be strong Mars and Venus aspects. When sexual appeal is mistaken for love we would expect Mars and Venus connections but little else to hold the charts together. Ascendant Mars and Venus together symbolize sex.

The connections to do with attraction will be more fifth house than seventh. For example the ruler of your fifth house may conjunct his fifth house cusp. Or your Mars or Venus may.

If the Synastry reveals all you have in common is sex. You than must then regard the relationship as an encounter, a thrilling love affair, that is to be enjoyed for its dazzling passion, and the experience it can give life. With this love you can live a little dangerously but do not try to build your or future life on it. Regard this as your adventure, and enjoy it all, the passion and the pain, and the joys ands sorrows, as you would enjoy a good film or book. You may feel for the characters and story in the film but they are not real and neither is this. This leaves you free, to continue relationship, but without blocking the way emotionally and psychically to the path that will lead to your true soul a mate.

We are bound sometimes bound more by the physical, than the mental, because the physical; has feelings that boarder on the ethereal too, and the emotions are aroused when we mistake or cannot separate then. We are bound more by illusion than truth.

A client, having realized there was no future in her relationship but being addicted to the confusion ecstatic sexual allure of it, and the space it gave her in life to dream in, asked me if she should find the strength to end the relationship, she hoped her soul mate might come sooner into her life if she did. She was hungry to experience this thrilling addictive state all again, reluctant to leave go of it, but wanted it, craved it to be satiated with the extra dimensions to her life and future. both worldly and unworldly that only the Soul mate could open up, and the security this time of knowing it would never end. In such cases the answer is often no, you should not end it, to realize that it must end is sometimes all the strength you need. To realize it is to be more than half way free. It is the change and realization we make inside our self that is more important to fate and karma than the external event. To end the relationship will not bring the soul mate into your life quicker. Unless something in the chart shows it will. Such a relationship may also have karmic purpose, of have to be got through and run its right course, even if that course is torturous before the true soul mate can come. Things cut short sometimes leave a residue of karma. It is better that everything end in its right time. For some people sex and love are quite separate The one can be had without the other. These people don't fall into the honey trap.

Love And Death

The sun and Moon are the Lights of life and when they are blotted out, there is a "threat" to life., (eclipses sometimes count too).

In a sick persons chart when the sun and Moon both become blocked by malefic, the sickness can turn deathly. Especially if one of the planets involved in the aspect are also the ruler of the house of death, but there is always a chance the person will survive, if their will, constitution, and care given to them is strong enough.

Here a "classic" example, Brian. This mans tragic death happened in a Scottish village in May 2006. He died by hanging. His story is also a love story, but not a happy one. He, died because he loved too much and felt he could not live without the one he loved. The women, Lilya, my client, had a long and volatile relationship with him spanning several years.

He was, morose, moody, drunken, violent and vile, but the involvement was an old one. It began under better circumstanced and over the years it deteriorated. On one occasion he broke three of her ribs, she left like an injured bird and went to live in a battered wives refuge. Lilya herself had violent provocative temper. She was Capricorn, practical, hardy and enduring, But each time she left, she returned to him, finding it hard to abandon a relationship that despite everything else that was wrong with it, did have love, it had its thorns and roses. For some people love chills, it freezes itself into the soul, with a realize that no matter how tortuous it is at times, no matter how many times you say you will walk away, there you stand, feet in concrete unable to go. No matter how often your walk away, you go back. It is not always weakness that drags someone back, it can be strength, or the inability to admit defeat.

Lilya finally found the strength to stand alone. She refused to forgive him or return to him. Too many nights when the sound of the key in the door, made fear clutch into the dark recess of her being. Too many memories. Too many failed attempts to haul the relationship from darkest well to which humanity can sink. Too tired.

After one final row and all the usual promises that life would be different this time. Lilya stood firm. Brian, defeated by her resolve was unable to find his own strength to continue alone.

Chart for Brian

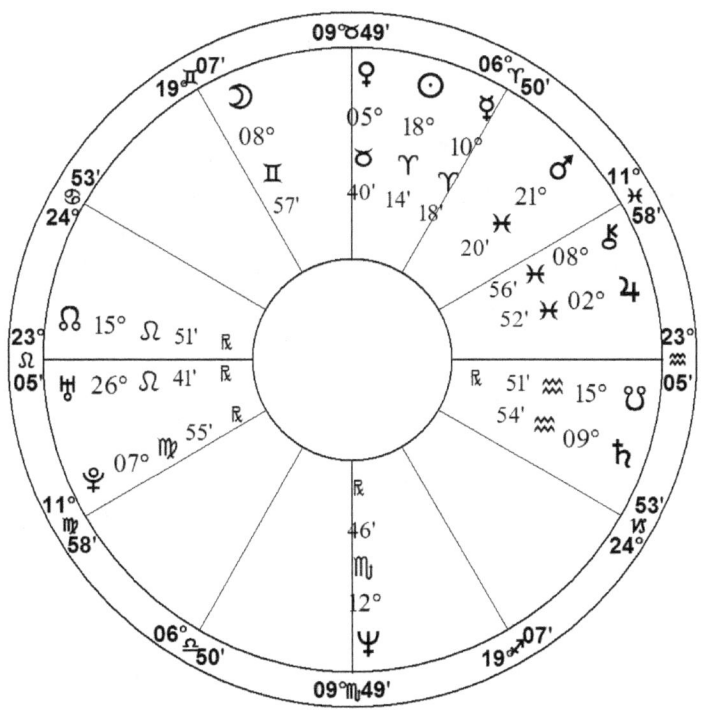

One evening after a fraught and desperate visit to her door to plead with her to have him back he, turned away from her house a final time. He took a rope from his van, climbed on a garden fence and hung himself from the arm of an antique lamp post that stood beside it, in ally a few yards behind her home. Its all in the chart. Transit and natal. The only thing differing from a classic case, is at the time of suicide the Moon was not afflicted. Though its badly placed in his natal chart, receiving hard aspects. The sun was afflicted by Venus. Not normally a malefic, but you'll see why it was malefic when you look at the charts.

Suicides have transit aspects. Its like a shadow that eclipse, or passes, over the life If someone's chart has this aspect they will feel depressed, all hope will seem lost to them, but if they resist the depression, the shadow recedes, life will get better if they can hang on. For suicide is like a shadow that falls over you, it gets to critical point, which may last a minute or an hour, a day, or longer, and that critical point is like a turning point between life and death, between mental disturbance, and peace. If you endure beyond that point, it recedes like the tide, like shadow. It doesn't have to happen. The same in assassinations or accidents, there is a critical moment, a psychological crisis point when it can change and life and death is decided.

In Brains chart his own ruling planet Mars is in the house of death. It suggests death by his own hands. His sun co rules the house of self undoing. The house of death being in Pisces, and containing Mars, and his

Neptune, ruler of the house death placed in the fourth house, all speak of mental instabilities of addictions, drugs or alcohol, as the second cause of his death..

Death Chart for Brian.

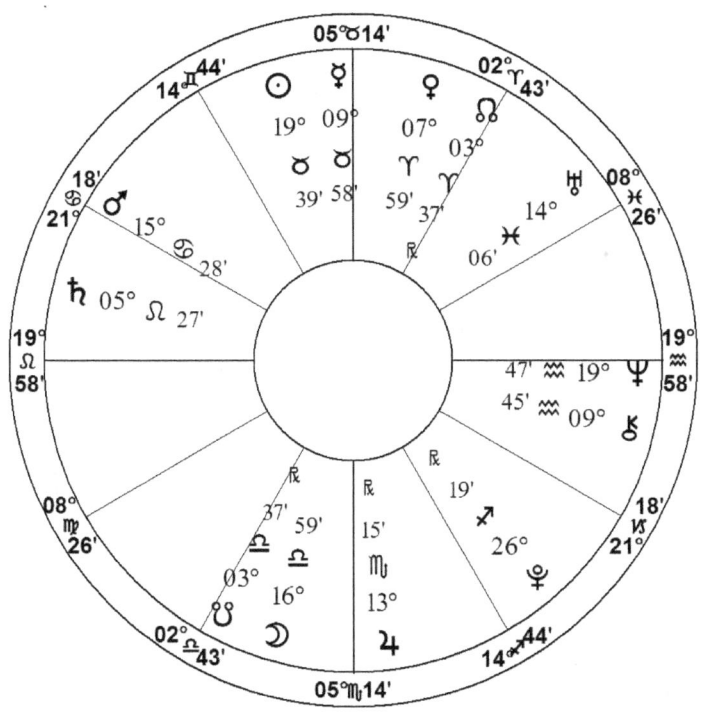

His sun rules part of his twelfth house, the house of self undoing. In some ways with Venus opposition his Neptune, Love was his only hope of being saved, from his addictions. It was his strength, (as well as being just another form of addiction). But Lilya the woman who did love him, though she tried so hard for many years, and endured more than most people could, she could not with stand the abuse of the relationship in the end. She had to save herself, and who would blame her. One life is as important as another.

She could not rescue him from his addiction, couldn't reform his abusive behavior, she had made too many sacrifices and couldn't be dragged down by love any more. He became a lost cause. The salvation did not come. He had tried hard to struggle against his problems for the sake of love, but always relapsed. like a drowning man falling back from the rocks into the sea. He slipped down lower and lower each time, until the sea surrounded him. He had love but he didn't have strength to save himself any more. Unlike Lilya who reached rock bottom and found her own strength. Brian was lost. In some ways we can only rescue ourselves, its not other people who save us. They only help, and often like Lilya it is at great cost to themselves. It is interesting to compare Brian's Natal chart with the transits on the day of his suicide. And interesting to compare his chart, the chart of a relationship destroyed by addictions, to the some of the charts of addictive love relationships, elsewhere in the book.

Of Death And Karma

In a future Volume we may look more closely at karma, past lives, reincarnation and relationships. In this one lets just look briefly at what the house of death can us at a glance.

Any planet in the eighth house will have an influence *after* marriage, or *after* the union has become permanent, but not usually *before* that. So when you have a planet in the eighth house, the courtship and love could be happy, but troubles will come after wards if the planet is a difficult or maligned one. The roots of such problem will be karmic and so less easy to resolve. The eighth house is an *After* house, while the sixth house is a *before* house.

Traditional astrology teaches if the ruling planet of your eighth house is in your seventh house, or visa versa your partner will not live as long as you. I have not always found this to be the case, so don't be unduly alarmed if you have this aspect, death always depends on many different aspects, never just one. The aspect means you have been linked together in past incarnations. Other traditions say it can mean a funeral happens, before the wedding takes place..

Fated Love
Definition Of Fate

An astrologer is always asked, can fate be changed? Also questions like what is Destiny? Do we have free will, do we have a choice at all or is it all predetermined, are the pleasure and pain of life all set out like a landscape through which we must walk, never deviating from that narrow path?. If a thing, an event, can be changed, doesn't that invalidate all prediction? Are karma and destiny the same thing?.

Let us explore or explain the nature of fate. Karma and

fate are not *quite* the same thing but they do work together. Our karma is decided before birth as a result of our previous life. Karma also determines our birth time and place. You could say that no matter how unfair life feels, we get the right chart or right fate at birth for our karma. Fate enforces the karma, we can improve our karma through working with the hard task that fate seems to heap on us. Fate is like a rope that binds us, have you ever taken a rope apart? It is comprised of many different fibrous strands, all woven into one rope. So that all we see is one rope, not the many strands that make it. We call this rope fate like it was a single thing.

It is important to understand fate is not single power, but a collection of things. Each of these fibers seems unchangeable, but taken separately they are not. One fiber is the effect of the subconscious mind, this is what makes us behave the way we do, it rules things we are not conscious of, what an analyst would call a behavior pattern, the way we deal with things, attitudes that have taken a lifetime to build up. These attitudes are a subtle as the lines on a face, but they determine how others will react to us. It can for example screw a situation up when we could have behaved different and succeeded. It can make a lover walk out of our life when he might have stayed. It can feel like fate, because haven't consciously said Go. But we have said it or turned him away in all the subtle ways. Other fibers that come together in this rope called fate, are things like Chance. Chance is when you are on a train and it crashes. Circumstance, which is the collective fate of a number of places and individuals coming together and the way on reacts on the other. Chance or Circumstance is the most difficult pattern to change. For while we can work on our fates and subconscious actions and those close to us, we cannot always work on the collective.

Yet your subconscious still chose that path of destructive chance,. The inner navigator of the soul, who determines whether we will take one path or another, whether we will be late, miss the train and miss the crash, by a moment, Whether we walk unknowingly into its dangerous path. There is a part of our subconscious that steers us. Nothing is really accidental..

There are other fibers too that merge to make what seems a binding rope of fate. are brought out and modified by other factors which are not fate but influence it. These include our own character. The famous phrase that character is destiny, is true. Destiny is the future, but it is also linked to the past,

A victims has a victims destiny, because it is all his soul has learned and all of fate and circumstance will seem to conspire to drag him back there, despite his struggle to be stronger. By undoing the things that bind us to our destiny, like finding the root cause. We can change not no only our self but a real change becomes visible in your daily life. The physical body limits or helps us, this is another of fates fibers, social class at birth, wealth, education or opportunity, these seem things we have very little control of. We are blessed or curse by them from birth., but individually if we *can* change them, not always radically, but to some extent.

Some are direct decisions, some subconscious. The subconscious ones will seem not like decisions at all but like a conspiracy of circumstance but they are really your own inner decision too, or lack of it,

The art of astrology has to do with predicting and analyzing this collective called fate, but it recognizes the persons actions efforts and decisions, conscious and subconscious can effect this fate. Or put simply Fate is not entirely fixed. How easy is it to change even one of these fibers in the ropes of fate?. Immensely difficult, but it can be done. First you must recognize the components and how you are stitched into the particular strand or piece of fate. Most people go through life without knowing how or why things happen. When we work with our fate or our own inner self we work with our karma too.

Venus Retrograde

Lets lighten the manuscript a little now and look at the effects of Venus when she is retrograde in the Natal chart.

Venus is the significator or love and if your born when Venus is retrograde in your chart, you are born at a disadvantage when it comes to finding love and friendship. If you have a retrograde venus, you will find the best soul mate or companion in someone who has a retrograde Mars in the same sign., or opposite signe. Or someone whos venus isnt retrograde but who shares your own Venus sign

Aries,

Venus retrograde in Aries makes you defensive, lonely and afraid of other peoples opinion of you. You run away from love, but experience the richness of life, You have brief encounters and many different worldly experiences, eroticisms and distractions, but too much self involvement prevents your finding real lasting love.

Taurus

You hunger after a past love, or the past always seem to have more to offer you than the present. There is a gap in your life and heart. But you also store up past hurts and blame the present love for what the past love has done. If the past love was unfaithful, you'll be destructively suspicious of the present one, even though it's a different person. This way you spoil your own chances.

Gemini.

Inwardly you at odds with yourself, the battle between who your are and what others expect you to be. You are a very good and fascinating friend, but friendship sometimes drowns out love, or your relationships fall down when you fail to make the transition from friendship to love.

Cancer.

In love you can seem needy, pestering and dependant and immature, tied to home and family.. In involvements there is never enough love for you. You demand too much, its as though you subconsciously seek a parent figure, not a partner Your karmic lessons are to love life a mature adult, not to seek love like a child.

Leo.

Karmic lesson are about power and lack of it. Subconsciously you test lovers to see how far you can go. Cruel games of cat and mouse. You want them to know you're the one running the relationship. You feel unappreciated you make too many sacrifices. You over react to things, you are difficult to love, you have a power complex.

Virgo,

You demand too much of yourself, self critical, blaming yourself, you put a strain on the involvement by focusing too much on faults and unhappiness too much on making things better, on investigating causes of unhappiness. You give too much of yourself, and You demand too much by demanding too little.

Libra

You are romantic, visionary in love, you want the dream of love, not the reality, You are unsure of what you want emotionally and sexually. Someone like you will always attract you, but is elusive, difficult to find. Its difficult for you to adapt to other people enough to love them, this is why you fantasize they are like you, or delude yourself they are. When you see through your own dream love fails.

Scorpio

You are soulful and secretive. You are a mystery, even to those who know you most. You feel that few people have ever understood you. You brood and dwell on things. You may seem frigid and unresponsive emotionally. Sexually discontented. You shop around too much for a better love, better life, you think you will find your ideal but you find what you seek within yourself, you wont find it without. Your karmic lesson are to learn to love and value yourself.

Sagittarius

You guard your freedom, afraid that commitment means being imprisoned by love. You are an adventurer, afraid of missing out on life and love, and all the world capers it has to offer. The future has more attraction than the present, many short lived encounters and relationships, will be yours but in the end a lonely path, you don't remain long enough in any one relationship to put down roots.

Capricorn

You keep your life and thoughts closed. You are afraid to seem vulnerable, or foolish in love. You attract relationship where you feel you are more in love with the person than they are with you, You live too much lingering over past loves, who are gone, and relationships that seem to be incomplete, or left unfinished. Your karmic lessons are to live in the present.

Aquarius.

You scatter you affections, your love and friendship like crumbling of bread to the birds, feeding so many people. You like freedom, passion and the taste of love, but having just one love, doesn't appeal, to others you seem unconventional, cool, impersonal, past rejections, make you afraid to love, and make you difficult to reach.

Pisces

You feel separated from thus you could love, by invisible bonds. You are impressionable, you live too much in fantasies of love, the look in a personas eyes the smile on their lips, but reality passes you by or doesn't match your hopes and leave you lonely. You are unrealistic about love and sex, and retreat into your dreams, the more you allow illusion to seep into reality, the more it separate you from others, and finding love.

Venus retrograde

Venus Retrograde may sometimes speak of an unusual Interest in Love and relationships. If you have a retrograde. Love doesn't fool you with its mysteries yet you are intensely fascinated on some level by all intimate relationships. Sexually and Socially you do not fit into the Mainstream or broad high way of life, As I said previously, some people with Venus retrograde do become celibate, or virtually so, frigid or self denying; Others do the opposite, and become Satyrs and nymphomaniacs who dwell in a mansion of sexuality but like their repressed inhibited counterparts they lock the door on love. It is two sides of the same coin. There is always something both hidden and extreme about a retrograde Venus. It can alternate over the years between Abstention and promiscuity, earthly love and spiritual love depending on the transits in the chart aspecting Venus. Some astrologer think that when a transit aspects a retrograde Natal planet, the natal it has no, or very little influence., Retrograde planet always turn direct at some point in life. This can cause reversals of the previous state. The vigorous ones find when the fire burns out they turn from a rampaging youth to a virtuous nun like old age. The virginal prudish ones one day discover their own sexuality. Retrograde Venus in old age, or after they have made the transition to the opposite side of their Venus, at whatever age, are very good at mentoring and guiding and befriending younger versions of themselves through troubled relationships. They have seen both sides of the door, and have become unshockable, worldly wise, understanding, because their footsteps have taken them to places no one could ever guess at. Places no one else could ever know.

Occasionaly retrograde venus can form a critical piece of an Afflicted chart, where the person has been maltreated or,abused, betrayed in love or had traumatic experiences at the hands of those they have loved. Venus retrograde can represent an old wound from this life or from a past incarnation. These people cannot reach out or show the love they feel, or ask for the love they need, quite so well or easily as others.

If you have Retrograde Venus, s times goes on you may fear that you will never marry or find a permanent relationship. You will, and the marriage can be happy but it can seem odd and untraditional to others.

Venus retrograde by transit, in the opposite sign to where Venus was at birth, has the reverse effect of all this and promotes your, love life, pushes things forwards brings happy outcomes to romantic situations To a lesser extent Venus retrograde and opposite to the Sun, but transit can bring love and friendship into focus better. The following signs are opposite each other. Aries is opposite to Libra. Taurus is opposite to Scorpio. Gemini is opposite to Sagittarius, Cancer is opposite to Capricorn. Leo is opposite Aquarius and Virgo is opposite Pisces.

Venus Stationary
The station of venus in a natal chart acts like a bolder of stone that nothing can shift. Impervious to time, it can either give a very long enduring happy marriage when benficialy placed and aspected in the chart; or it can act like a total block to prevent a love relationship or marriage taking place or moving beyond a certain point, when adversely aspected. A stationary planet is a stuck planet. There will be more about stationery planets in my advanced books of Soul mate.

The Happy Couple
The two charts reproduced here belong to a Gay male couple who have lived together for many years. Their time together has been like an echo of the church marriage vows, taken by most English married

couples, " for richer, for poorer, for better for worse, in sickness and in health," also "to love and to cherish".

In a recent letter I was told Gavin's life had been made utterly miserable by bullying and persecution at work, to the point where the victimization became intolerable and he suffered a nervous break down. As a result he, had to leave work and could no longer contribute much to the household finances. David, a property manager has also had financial problems, which had brought him to the verge of suicide, but he had to stay strong for Gavin. Gavin's loss of employment added to that burden, and caused him to contact me after an absence of many years. I knew David before he met Gavin. Like most people when he first came to me, he wanted his soul mate chart done. That reading had predicted Gavin in every detail. At the time of writing to me he felt he felt close to the end, but the one constant and enduring beacon of strength and happiness that has helped both men to survive human cruelty, inhumanity, and the struggle against financial wreckage is their abiding love for each other.

The essential thing about the true soul mate is that while the tides of misfortune and injustice can bring you down to your knees. They do not divide you, you unite against the savage winter of your despair and are not swept away by it. There is the strength that comes from no longer being alone in the cold face of adversity. If your love cannot survive in spite of sorrow than it is not a soul mate love. Not a greater love, though it may be a lesser love which still has its place in your life.

When we look a Gavin and David's charts. There are many hallmarks of the soul mate aspects previously discussed in both the books. This is why I have chosen to illustrate their charts, not so much as an exercise in Synastry, but as an example of a perfect match.

There is a connection between the eighth house, the house of death and reincarnation in both charts, that occurs in a multiple of ways. Gavin's eighth house is ruled by Neptune, which conjuncts David's Venus.

From this conjunction we get an insight into how delightful and beautiful the encounter between them felt. Venus being the planet of love, Neptune being an almost mystical bond, that can make the senses drunk with love. This planet also being the planet of foreigners. David was born in Cyprus and Gavin in Wales, two very different countries and cultures.

In David's chart, his eighth house ruler is Venus, the planet of love, which conjuncts Gavin's Neptune. The two charts reflect each other like a mirror. (this kind of aspect is known in astrology as a form of " mutual reception ") These mutual aspects hint at a karmic bond, and point to the two being soul mates. There are powerful Venus Neptune aspects in the Synastry between the charts, falling in the constellation of Scorpio, the sign of hidden things, it is an indication that the love was once secret, and kept in the shadows, that it was like powerful waking dream. At First at the start of the relationship David feared his love might not be reciprocated.

Chart for David

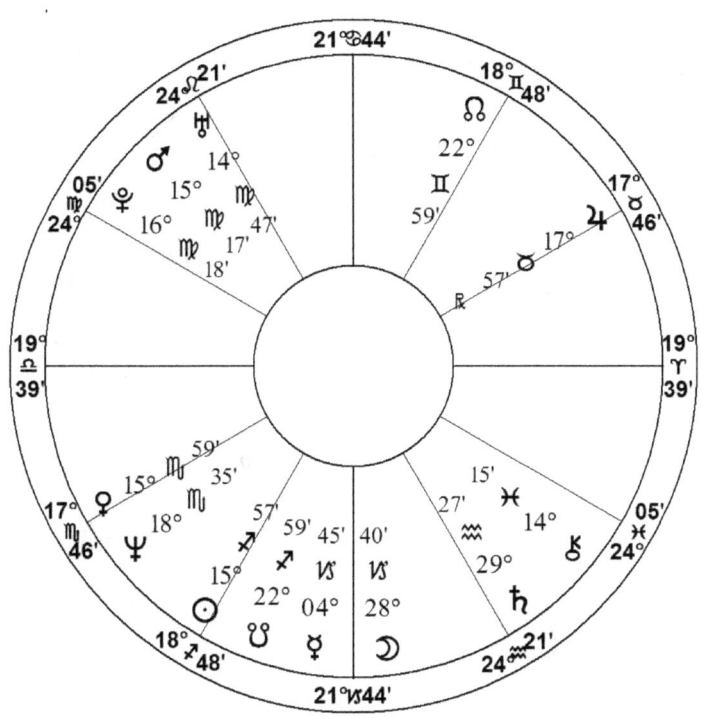

But since these aspects and connections are formed in both charts, this dream finally possessed them both and it took root, and it was mutual. Mutual aspects are anchored in reality. If there is love or infatuation but no chart connection, then it is a dream. When we have

Neptune aspects we must be very careful for Neptune too can be illusion.

Chart for Gavin

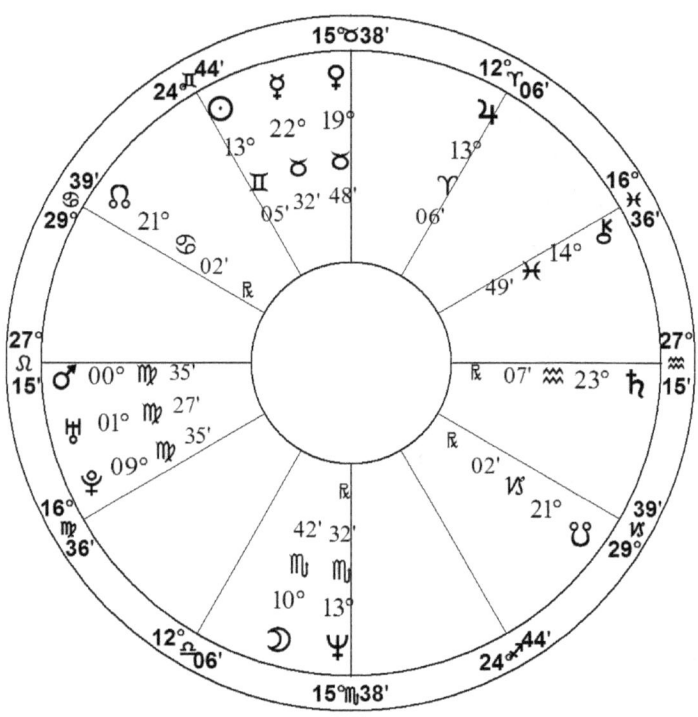

We must always ascertain if it its a love that can be more than a hope or a prospect, if it is one that is destined to materialize into a future?, because so often Neptune is a beautiful mirage, an elusive wrap of unrealistic feelings and thoughts and mistaken perceptions that can cling to the mind regardless of reality, and not allow us to see truth or daylight.

Neptune can be fragile, but because Gavin's Jupiter conjuncts David house of marriage, it roots the prospect of love more into reality. Jupiter conjuncting the marriage house cusp is a common aspect in charts where the two, become lovers, and usually where they get married, or set up home.. It helps make the more dreamy Neptune love aspects materialize into something solid and substantial

Gavin's Neptune opposes David Jupiter, adding weight to the aspects. Jupiter of course is the co ruler of Gavin's eighth house, which is why in this chart we are so interested in Jupiter. In this chart it, symbolizes the soul mate link or past life karma between them materializing or culminating in a " marriage" in the present life.

David's chart shows his Saturn conjunct to Gavin's house of marriage. Jupiter is the plant of Joy and Saturn the planet of caution and longer term associations. Saturn can also be the planet of delays sorrows and endings. But since Saturn is co ruler of Gavin's seventh house it takes on its most positive aspect. In astrology a ruler always manifest as positive, even in a bad aspect it will milk what positive qualities it can from the aspect, Stature in this chart then tells of endurance, faithfulness, waiting, and reliability, its not its negative shadow of partings and tears. Saturn means there is a willingness to put work and effort into the marriage and home. Saturn earths this relationship in reality. Gavin's

Jupiter brings joy into David's life, These two aspect balance each other. Both men have Mars in the same zodiac sign. Mars is ruler of David's marriage house. Mars is conjunct Uranus in each persons chart. in an Earth sign. Again Earth signs help pull a relationship down to reality. This mutual aspect is again like an extra velvet ribbon binding the gift of marriage together, since Uranus and Mars are both the primary marriage house rulers of the two charts. These are only the most obvious of the soul mate aspects, if you study the two charts you can find many more.

Now to move back to David and Gavin's history, to the time when they first met. Uranus is the planet of sudden and changing circumstances, it also traditionally symbolizes divorce or "broken up partnerships" Being prominent in the relationship aspects of both charts can mean meeting ones soulmate at a time when one relationship has to end before the new one can begin.

I recall when David was first my client. He was living in London and had consulted me for a Career reading at the time. I persuaded him to have his soul mate chart done too, for I intuitively felt that love was not far away from for this man. I would not have described David as hungry to settle down at the time, rather the reverse, as will be seen from the quincunx between his seventh house cusp and his Mars Uranus Pluto stelium in the house of friendship. This set of aspects would suggest a man who had many fascinating friends, new acquaintances, and short lived interesting unions (Uranus). One who would have several relationships, sexual encounters, adventures and close friendships. (Mars) before he found the right man.

The Soul mate, (Pluto aspect) would totally alter his life and his character. He would become settled and faithful (seventh house). The aspect between the stelium and the cusp being a stress aspect, indicates that past relationships had left a legacy of emotional wounds, scars on the soul at that time. This is probably why David did not seem to want to get involved with others except on a superficial level. David always seemed so "Footloose and Fancy Free" as the phrase goes. Forever young, Changing jobs, changing friends constantly. But hating to be on his own. The trine between the stelium and retrograde Jupiter forecast an ideal relationship would emerge in later life that would heal the wounds of the past (Chiron aspect Chiron is the healer). Later life being some point after age thirty five, because Jupiter is retrograde.

Gavin was not known to me. Gavin was the man I had predicted in David's Soul mate chart, but when David and Gavin met, Gavin was the boyfriend of a mutual friend of theirs, and the relationship remained simply a friendship. They were all part of a wide circle of friends. The crumbs of love David got were what fell to him as an acquaintance who stood in the sidelines of the circle and dared not speak his growing love, it remained very much distant for a year or more, until the winds of time began to change and all the friends the relationships broke up. The fate that had brought them, and the other friends in the group together was fast falling apart.

They were all much traveled people in this group. One worked for an air line and was never at home. One was emigrating to marry her lover, One had a second home. Another landed a prime job in a different place and left. None of them lived permanently in country of their birth, Like the tide they were washed up together and when the tide changed they were washed apart amid the chaos changing jobs, and universities and marriages and houses and precarious addresses and crumbling hopes and soaring hearts This had been David's way of life. Gavin and David went their separate ways. So did the others

They agreed to all meet up in ten years time, if they all lost touch, a rendezvous in Sydney harbor on the night of the millennium with all the other mutual friends from that era in their lives, when the whole world was celebrating the new year. I don't know if that promise was ever kept, I would imagine very many people promised old friends, fellow students, and drifting family acquaintances and old loves the same thing around the world, for the millennium was still many years ahead then. Life is divided into chapters, into personal eras that never come again. At certain times we are aware of this. Such moments are special. We take someone's hand we know it is for the last time, though we don't know why or how, or what has ended, just that it has or will. We try to recapture the moment, but like a photograph it is gone changed,. Never will that moment come again. We promise to meet but we don't. For David this was such a time.

Some people know when they approach the end of a chapter, most go blindly on believing that life is continual. They cannot draw the end of a chapter exactly by hindsight. In David's case the friends parted in a restaurant by the Thames, with toast of white wine, they were still all young, mostly unattached, , with the vitality, joy, the hope and wonder of youth.. unburdened by the scars and cynicism and hardship coldness of heart life can bring as you get older and the struggles get harder. Gavin had not had his break down, David hadn't had his nightmare debts neither had faced suicide or the death of loved ones head on. They were not yet lovers, life's promise still awaited them, they were happy to move with the flow of the wind, but aware at that night, parting under starry skies in a London street, to walk home or get into taxi, that life might not ever bring them together again. So to meet at the millennium, in a particular place at the stroke of midnight was like a pact.

I think David would have waited a thousand years, another millennium if he'd had to for Gavin's love! Saturn is the planet of endless time and his Saturn conjuncts Gavin's marriage house and Gavin's own Saturn. The delay, the slow beginning of the relationship, the duty to others, the relationship that had to end before theirs could begin, its all in that planet, Yes they both would have waited.

I don't know what happened on the year two thousand and whether the reunion was kept. I never ask my clients to reveal anything, they tell me only what they choose. I never ask questions. Some write letters as long as books, some only write a few words. I know what I'm meant to know, only what fate wants me to know, to do their reading, nothing more. What I do know dear reader, is destiny or love which is perhaps the same thing, can never keep two soul mates apart. It was far before the millennium that Gavin David re met, and now its long, long after the millennium and they are still together the perfect couple.

Changing The Fate Of Love
Can a bad love destiny be changed, and how?

Some astrologers, and some clients, are extremely fatalistic. They believe that nothing can be changed, that we are set on earth to endure our fate, regardless of whether it brings joy or suffering; because the road we travel is our fixed karma. Where we must pay for our misdeeds, and make amends, and be rewarded for good behavior. It is true that fate, or what appears to be pre destined is sometimes hard to change, but it is not impossible, and when the days of life get dark we must keep this in mind. Change is part of existence. The winter will turn to spring. There is another way of looking at it. The astrology chart is a kind of map to find our way through life, some things cannot be changed, like an eternal essence that remains always there, but by reading it, we can either take a hard path of an easier one. even within that essential core of our life we can change some things, and the things outside that essential core karma, we can change more radically.

In future volumes we may look at deeper ways to change a bad karma or turn and unlucky destiny in love and life around. The key to personal happiness, happiness, and sublime love is kept within each of our charts, we just have to unlock it. Here I will show you one simple basic way of changing a difficult love destiny, and I will illustrate it with a client chart and case history. Every planet has three faces. They are like the three fates in mythology. One is its negative, a downcast evil side which is like a road full of darkness that we inadvertently turn into on a dim rainy night and can't quite find our way back. And that same planet has a positive or daylight side, that can uplift our hearts, a plate of joy and abundance that is served to us, so we can feast ourselves. It also has a neutral side, that is neither good nor bad, but like a building at the structure of life its just there. Some people seem to always to choose the happy door, others walk through the door to the dark side. Most of us do a bit of both. The example is a female client, Erina.

As you can see from her chart the ruling planet of her house of soul mates falls in the twelfth house. The house of sorrows. She had a history of short involvements with attractive personable but deeply unstable men. The first was a semi alcoholic, who couldn't pull himself out of the pit. Note the unhappy ruler of her seventh is not only in the house of difficulty, but falls opposite Neptune, the planet of addictions.

He was only sober for about three days out of seven. Through Neptune retrograde in Scorpio, gave him the ability to conceal his addiction when they first met. The next man in her life was in the middle of a nervous breakdown when they met. He never quite recovered. Another was a chronic suicidal depressive. (Note Sagittarius rules both the house of soul mates and the house of death, and the afflicted addicted Jupiter. Sagittarius like sports. He was a man addicted or at least attracted toward playing dangerous games with suicide or death) Every man Erina met had a fatal destructive flaw, and became wholly dependant on her (Neptune dependencies) to prop up their lives and keep them on an even keel. They wore her out with work and worry, dragged her down into a life that was basically going nowhere.

She had a twelfth house Moon, ruler of her fourth, both cuspal and difficult. Showing some difficulty with the role of mothering. Which is perhaps one of the deeper karmic reasons that fate had drawn men who needed care to her. Erina badly wanted to have a baby, but the men she met were not stable enough to be a father or husband. They were, she said, like babies themselves; clinging, demanding. hopeless and helpless. Bring up a child alone was not an option Erina had to work for her living (Saturn, retrograde, opposing house of children and ruling house of Career, which translates as a child delayed because the woman cannot give up her Career)..

The twelfth is one of institutions, and unstable damaged people. The Jupiter Neptune aspect and the twelfth house Moon represents the suffocating dependency of such people as partners and the subterranean mother substitute theme. We decided that this was her destiny. Her fate to always come into contact with these types. That on some level she had to learn to accept and work with this fate, because she had a subconscious gift to give these people, a talent to prop up and mend their unhappy lives. Which was what was happening in her personal life.

Chart for Erina

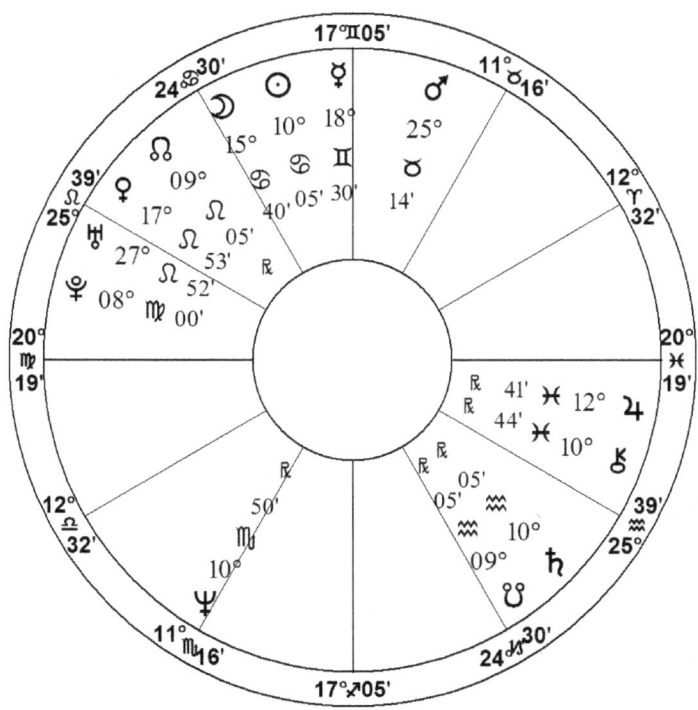

This isn't as bleakly dismal as it sounds. We decided that maybe she could "offload " this fate into a different area of her life. By going to work in an actual institution. A prison or hospital. That this might shift all the negative energies of the chart into the twelfth house, in a practical way. And so leave the seventh house love and relationship area of her chart free to meet the decent responsible well balance man ordinary she'd always wanted.

The other way of offloading the fate, might have been to bravely go ahead have a child, despite the struggle of brining it up alone. So that she was substituting the dependant childish men, for a real child, which she wanted anyway. Thus again leaving the fate of the future relationship free to find a better man. But her Saturn aspect and the practicalities of her life blocked this avenue or option more heavily. A change in career, (Saturn opposite Uranus, in fifth house, house of children, Saturn ruler of Midhaven) would be beneficial to the part of her that wanted a child. Might later lead to having a child as well as a man.

This worked well for Erina. She got a job in an open mental clinic hospital, which housed mainly young women with eating disorders. They were mostly Bulimic, which is interesting when you think the Moon is the planet of nurturing, feeding, caring. While Jupiter in Taurus is linked with over eating. She was able to use this nurturing part of her character to prop up the lives of patients. She found it satisfying, though at first the last thing she had wanted in her life was more responsibility. Her life began to automatically turn around. Her nurturing supportive skills were given to young girls, not men, and in her personal life she met fewer unstable men. The boyfriends improved, though she had yet to meet her soulmate. Two years passed before she did. The important thing to note is that her fate was re-channeled into a better direction.

The soul mate was much as her chart aspects described. He was rotund (Jupiter in Taurus) He wore round glasses with a brown frame (Moon and Luna nodes aspecting the seventh also Neptune opposing Jupiter suggest glasses, poor eyesight. It is Moon Aries that gives us the color and shape of the frame). He had a "Moon shaped " face and a pale rosy complexion (Aries Moon, Aries ruled by the " red" planet Mars) His hair in True Sagittarius fashion was beginning to thin and bald at the front and he had a hot head. But his hair was a nice shade of brown, cigar brown with just enough red tone in the Brown to brighten the shade. He was older than her. She described as him as cheerful or Jovial in character, (Jupiter in an earth sign), Down to earth, materialistic (Taurus) normal well balanced mentally and happy. He worked as a sales rep for a pharmaceutical (a drug) company. The company were well known for their anti depressants. Other than that neither drugs, depression or drink entered his life. Other Neptune Jupiter influences did. He traveled much, owned a small boat, fished and painted, liked horses, all positive Neptunian, Jupiter things.

So when an area of the chart or fate works very negatively it is possible sometimes to change the whole pattern of that fate. By changing your life very slightly. Its rather like getting the kaleidoscope pieces of your life to fall into a difference place where they fit better.

You keep the same pieces because you have no choice in that, but you arrange them into a better pattern. The result can be profound.

There are other deeper and more mystical ways of changing a destiny. In some case sheer will power can do it. The inner strength to haul yourself out of a hole., But the thing to know about fate and astrology, is no matter how negative it can seemed at times, the dark night of the soul may descend on you, but the chart is a map, it can show the road out to something better. Once you understand fate it is like a light in a dark room that illuminates much more. It empowers you. It is the key that can change your life from what you have, to what you want. Astrology is a magical art, it is about Mastering your destiny, not being its puppet. It is a mystical science that can transform your life.

Aspects That Deny Love

There is no chart that is totally unlucky or denies love completely. Who ever you are and wherever you are love will find you one day. For an astrologer the more difficult a chart is, the more fascinating it is. Some rare but unfortunate charts have what are called an "affliction" to the planets of love, or the house of marriage. This means a malefic planet aspecting the love planets, Venus, the Moon, or the ruler of the seventh house, or the house of marriage at birth. If a person has one affliction aspecting the marriage house, it reduces the chances of their finding a partner, or of having a happy future. If they have two or more afflictions it can make for a bad fate in love or marriage and disrupt events.

Traditional astrology tells us the sun in the seventh or first house is less likely to marry, that this is symbol of being self centered or married to the self. I do not count this as an affliction, but I have included it here since we are exploring aspects that deny love.

Traditional astrology also informs us that if you are born with the sun conjunct the Moon (Born at a new Moon, for sun conjunct Moon and new Moon are the same thing) if the conjunction is happily aspected by good planets, there will be good fortune and happiness in matters of love, but if the conjunction receives hard aspects from a malefic you can expect sorrow to dog your heels . Here are some other old rules.

If the sun and Moon are in square, at birth there is difficulty in adapting to the married state.

If Saturn is conjunct or in a hard aspect to the sun, Moon, or seventh house cusp or its ruler, and especially if Saturn is also badly aspected, or dominates the chart there is a lack of love. The soul builds up barriers, inhibitions, it cannot give or receive love so easily.

With Mars in malefic aspect to the sun Moon, or seventh house cusp there is danger of a relationship marred by violence or quarrels, especially if Mars is also in bad aspect to Saturn or Pluto.

Mars in considered malefic when he is in the second house, unless the second house is ruled by Mercury.. He is also said to be a malefic influence bringing domestic troubles and family discord in the fourth house, unless he is co ruler of it, that is to say unless the fourth house is under Aries or Scorpio.

Again in the seventh house Mars can be difficult, unless in Capricorn or its opposite Cancer. An afflicted or malefic Mars increases the possibility of separation or discord and violence in marriage.

Mars is malefic in the eighth house, when the eighth house isn't in Pisces or Sagittarius and in the twelfth house, when the twelfth isn't I ruled by Venus.

The prospect of a bad Mars is improved if the partner also has a malefic Mars, it doesn't cancel it out, but it harnesses the Mars energies towards a common task, so that the pair fight less, they fight the world instead of each other and find a mutual goal to focus on, like bringing up a child or running a business together. The danger then comes in later years with retirement, or when the children fly the nest, love can seem to end because and there is no longer anything to bind the negative energies into anything positive.

Venus in square or opposition to Saturn in a mans chart. And Mars in square or opposition to Saturn in a woman's chart, often delays or partly deny love and make romantic relationships disappointing, the spirit is often too sensitive not robust enough to cope with the rebuffs, rejections and hurts that often come in youth and so it has a struggle to open up to love in maturity. Mars was considered weakened or restrained by Saturn's power in such an aspect. Remembering that Mars is also the sexual energies, the vitality in a woman's chart. Mars is the kind of man she is physically attracted too, Saturn weakness, damps down or denies, he inhibits or obstructs the attraction for whatever reason.. In older astrology books this was known as the Old Maids aspect. These are only a handful of the malefic aspects or afflictions. More frightening still is the "Widow Maker " aspect, which we may come to in a more advanced book.

Most charts have both malefic and benefic aspects when it comes to love, so we must not judge a marriage unfit, or useless or think it will turn to ash and cinders because of t one bad aspect

I have to say that no chart ever denies love totally, it is my belief that, there is someone special for everyone., we each have our counterpart in this world. No chart is really so bad, no matter how afflicted it is, no matter what difficult aspects it holds, it is only a picture of a fate that has become distorted so that love becomes a misalliance, or road ending in nothing. Astrology has the knowledge that can redirected the path towards a positive outcome for you. Astrology is about prediction but its also about strengthening your character, and turning fate to your advantage.

Never despair no matter what suffering you have been through in the past., no matter how sad a way a relationship has ended., never despair. True love, is always stronger than false love and can set us free from illusion and false ties. No unhappy existence is ever hopeless nor its sorrows endless. The time will come when the soul mate walks into our life and all the shadows fall away. Never close your heart to love or life. Even if your heart has gone cold and withered like a winter bud that cannot bloom and open to love, it is only sleeping, any dormant., True love can wake it, true love can wash s way your loneliness it can conquer all your fears that have cause you to lock away your hopes and emotions and your heart form others. If you are afraid to reach out from the walls you have built and be hurt again, true love will reach inward and gently demolish all resistance, it will bring healing and renewal.

Karmic Astrology.

All our lives the subconscious builds an image of the ideal partner, or soul mate. All our lives we are guided towards this person by some mysterious force that is not yet love, but memory of past lives or a creed of inner knowledge denied to our conscious., it guides us through different loves and different pathways. This image is made from fragments of your life like a work of art in the mind. Until it becomes an inner invisible picture that is hidden from you, a collage of many fragments from your subconscious. It sketches in the absence in your life and leads you towards the day you will meet the soul mate.

Past lives, can guide us to future loves. This chart is of Tim. He is a school teacher in an archeology and history. His hobby or greatest obsession is historic battles. Particularly the battle of the Somme. He is often as depressed by it as much as he is drawn to it.

Chart for Tim

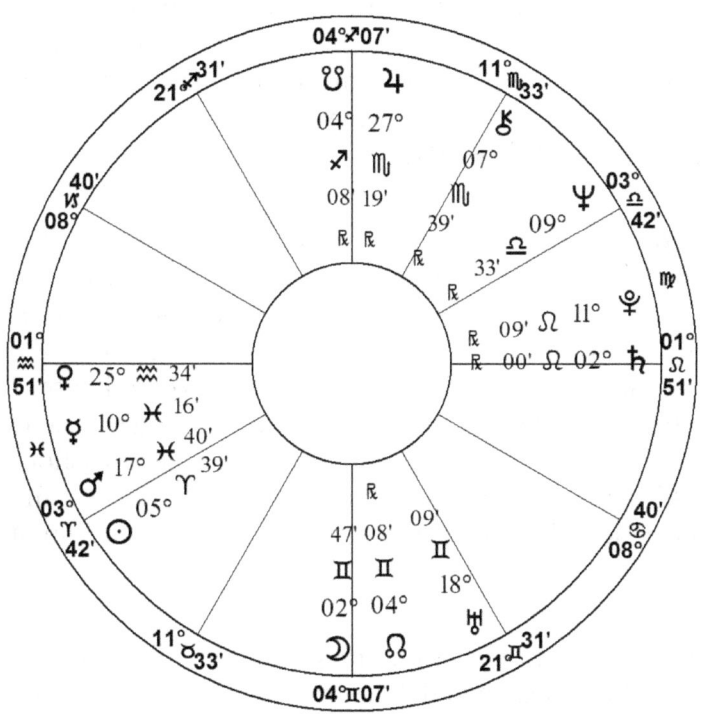

Tim told me this particular battle wouldn't let him go. Fascinated by it, he even dreamed a terrible recurrent nightmare where all he could see was mud, he was waist deep in mud and rain and barbed wire. A black shape as big as a house bearing down on him. " This obsession has poisoned my mind," he said." I cannot rest. I occupy my hours with others things but in every quiet time my mind turns back to study this one historic battle." He has Pluto in his seventh house. Pluto like Mars rules wars, but more especially in war it's the planet of the enemy. Had Tim been born in a different country or at an earlier time in history,, we might have predicted a marriage for him taking place during the war years. As it is it means a marriage that will transform his life utterly.

Pluto is the planet of the subconscious, the underground the mythical dark kingdom beneath the earth, Pluto is research, He also has Saturn, here, illustrating his interest in history and researching the past, and because the plants are in his seventh house. I predicted a soul mate who would share these same interests, this was also what he was subconscious looking for, compelled I think by an unknown past life connection. Tim met the woman I described to him at an archeological dig.

I was able to predict what she would look like from the chart. She is lean and delicate in looks, as suggested by Saturn, with mesmeric dark eyes, that are an unusual mix of dark grey and jet, clear and glossy they seem to dominate her face like jewels, and masses of fair hair. She was as striking and charismatic as Pluto would suggest. Had Mars cast an aspect we would have had a reddish blond, but he doesn't. the sun does and

Neptune does so we know her hair is long flowing,(Neptune) pure yellow or honey gold, and Neptune adds a delicately refinement and willowyness to her figure and her looks. A kind of, other worldly quality almost. Sandy, as she was called, had the look of the past about her. Tim said she had a stunning effect on him, that left him speechless as predicted (note mercury's angle to retrograde Pluto, is a hard one, and its a silencing one,)

Sandy liked antiques, of various eras, including war time memorabilia, but mostly vintage clothes and old posters. The battle of the Somme had no special allure for her at all.. but Hearing of Tim's interest, she'd given him a book about the Somme, that had by chance come into her possession. She also had a recurrent dream just before meeting Tim, of pushing someone in a wheel chair whose face she could not see. This dream was not as odd as it sounds, for Sandy, Tim's soul mate is a nurse who works with people with spinal injuries, this shows in his chart too, it is there for you to find if you look.

In the photo Tim showed me, Sandy had a curiously early English 1900- 1930s style, or way of platting and pinning her hair up to keep it out of the way during a dig. She wore wide black dusty trousers that resembled a long ankle skimming skirt. Edwardian style ankle boots. No make up, and only a tight string of pearls or small beads at her neck and an enigmatic smile, that spoke of other times other worlds. One could almost picture her belonging to 1916, the year of the Somme. more than the present day.

Barely had he met her when his obsessive interest in the Somme began to diminish. It was still a fascination but it faded back into its proper place in his life, note both planets are retrograde, sending a kind of reflex action to the ascendant. The ascendant is ones birth and beginnings and mercury the ruler of his house of dearth and reincarnation aspects Pluto as does the sun, which is the self, so we begin to see a strange unique pattern, the possibility that Tim may indeed have died in the Somme, or at any rate during some other battle (Note Mars the god of war opposite his house of death). Or perhaps he lived through it, forever traumatized and then met his soul mate.. It would not surprise me if Sandy was a nurse in her previous life too, A sweetheart left behind, before he went to fight. working in a military hospital. If they met after the battle that Tim's subconscious equates with the Somme. Maybe she did push him in a wheelchair.

Mars being in Pisces a watery sign makes me doubt the battle was actually the Somme. Though the mud and drenching rain he dreamed of might equate with Pisces. This is pure speculation. But wherever or whenever it was, there was a battle field, a field of death and a traumatic memory strong enough to survive the transition from life to death and back through rebirth to return at a critical time in nightmare form.

When a soul is reborn the memory is wiped clean. When Tim was reborn he may have retained a residue of the subconscious memory of this battle. Something working its way to the surface that had become ever more pressing and urgent as the years went on. More insistent as he came close to the time in this life when it would connect with the past life and he'd meet his same soul mate. In the past incarnation he must have met her before or after the battle. So that in his mind war was wrapped like a paper, like a backdrop all round the memories of this love of her. This soul mate, who he has searched for unknowingly all his life. Having found her my guess is the subconscious memory that had generated the intense interest in war, becoming obsessive directly they met, had served its purpose. So his interest in the battle declined, receded into the background of life once more. In this life he found her, in the past life he may have lost her then at the same time of year.

Tim met Sandy through archeological rather than war interests in the summer of 1974, they married in November 1975 (Tim's Saturn return, symbolic of cycle of time) Archeology is about digging up the past, literally with hands picks and shovels. The war interest, digging intellectually through the past in books and pictures. Tim's choice of vocation, the history teacher, is one of keeping the past alive. It is as though his life more then most peoples, was always attuned into looking for something, or someone, in the past..

The Garden Of Love

How to create your own psychic soul mate garden. A garden for the spirit of love to grow. In herbalism it has long been known that plants have curative properties. But what can heal the body can also heal the soul. To plant a soul mate garden is like planting a healing garden or a psychic garden it is complicated, and very individual. It is rather like a form of Feng-Shui but much more so. It takes into account your own individual astrology chart and the age old knowledge of astrological plants. But just as Zodiac sign astrology is like a fragment of the real thing, so here is some zodiac sign hints on making the garden that attract love and will suit your soul. It will encourage your soul mate to come into your life, and create a space for you to share.

In making a garden of love you should base the planting fragrances and flowers around your Venus and Mars signs most. As these symbolize love and passion, and Then your zodiac sign, or ruler, as this sign or planet represents you. You need to know your ruling planet and. also its opposite planetary influences. For we want to combine all these things in a practical way in planting our Soul mate psychic garden.

Taurus and Libra are both ruled by Venus, The trees and bushes of Venus have beautiful heavily scented flowers that hang in abundance, often white or pink. Pink is a Libra colour. They have pleasant sweet fruits and feminine fragrances and smooth glossy leaves. So if you were born under Libra or Taurus try planting flowering apple, apricot, cherries peach, strawberries Rowan and sycamores. The rowan (also called mountain ash) is a protective tree. I have one in my back yard to protect the back of the house from thieves vandals and intruders.

In the midst of the Taurus Libra garden you must blend plants belonging to its opposite, the planet Mars. You can find Mars plants in the next paragraph. If you know your Venus sign, plant something that is Venusian but partakes in some way of the nature of that sign. For instance if you are a Libra and have Venus in cancer, a watery sign that rules white flowers, you would planet the palest most delicate shades of pink flower, to mingle the Libra cancer qualities, and you'd choose a plant that likes moist ground but spread up into the air, not a ground covering plant for Cancer is Water and Libra air.

Mars ruled people, or Aries and Scorpio.

Trees and plants that belong to Mars are those which have thorns, prickles, sharp or pungent odors most red plants and those with conical tap root. Cactus and succulents, include at least one dark and favorite kind of pine tree, the lovely rose, the quince. Aries can feel at peace in a light open Japanese or Spanish garden with sand gravel, wood chips and different textures., But Scorpios soul will be happier in an English garden, or under Russian vine and overhanging shady spaces. And with some water in the garden. This is because Scorpio is also ruled by Pluto as well as mars.

Amongst these Aries Scorpio planets we must also place its opposite the planets of Venus.

Lets come to Jupiter with a few clews now. Jupiter, who is a Sagittarius and Pisces ruling planet. He owns plants are large and conspicuous, edible, have warm and pleasant odours, cruciform in shape and markings. They include fig plants for indoors, or warm walls, the date, oak, the lime tree. Pisces should have fountains and ponds because it is also ruled by Neptune Sagittarius some stately ornament.

In the Jupiter garden we must include Mercury ruled plants to spiritually draw the soul mate into our life.

Mercury ruler of Gemini and Virgo.

Mercurial plants have fine delicate frondy leaves, or alternatively tiny little leaves, and stems, and subtle smells. The myrtle the mulberry the bamboo. Archways and arbors, bowers and pergolas and overhead plants are all favored in this garden. and plant pots or hanging baskets both sides of the door Gemini's. Gemini is the twins, so everything must be balances, or at the same plant put at both sides ,it needs climbing plants while Virgos the other mercury ruled sign are happiest in a bird friendly garden that attracts, hedgehogs, squirrels and wild life. For our soul mate garden we must blend the plants under Pisces and Sagittarius into this arrangement, to create an affinity.

Saturn rules Capricorn and co rules Aquarius.

The plants of Saturn are have dull grey or green foliage, scaly textures or bark can be poisonous, or associated with funerals, but they needn't be sad or somber. The garden for your soul needs winter plants and evergreens in it. In the midst of this we need the opposite, the Moon and sun ruled plants to kindle the soulmate. Aquarius rules modern cultivars, sculpture, design, structured gardens. Gardens that are striking and different.

The Moon, and the sign of cancer. rules trees rich in sap. Plants with soft juicy thick leaves, pale often white flowers, water loving plants. Night scented plants. The rubber plant, the aloe. The olive palm trees privet, maple. The white Lilly. A still garden pool to meditate near. Born under Cancer, and you must blend the Saturn plants into your garden to attract your soulmate.

The sun, ruler of Leo. Golden and orange fruit, plants that have rounded leaves or rounded flowers, large and aromatic. They include the sun flower in all its varieties, the marigold the walnut and the vine. To attract the soul mate, when the sun is your ruler, you need Uranus ruled plants, which are strange and showy, unusual plants and modern sculptures and art works in the garden are all Uranus.

Your own garden of love will be influenced by your individual chart. Someone with Saturn strongly placed garden, regardless of their sign will probably like a traditional an old garden that is mature, with private places and tall walls. A garden that has mature trees and plants A garden to heal the past. If you had a strong Saturn then choosing a tree with white flower, or growing a white climbing rose up the tree or walls will help the karma of the garden. The tree will bring the element of the Moon, its opposite, a soul mate element into the garden..

The more you learn about astrology the more intricate and powerfully you can create your garden of love. A twelfth house Venus for instance will want a romantic kind of secret love garden with a private seat. Growing red, orange, puce or carmine and gold flowers, Mars flowers planted near it will then brings the soul mate into to your romantic corner. If your mars is in Aries, then these will be crimson or scarlet. The more you know the more elements you can include and the more magical your enchanted garden of love will be.

All I am giving you at this moment are a few hints a few notes from the book of time, all things on earth are connected. Not everyone is interested in gardening, but if you're an astrologer you should be interested in everything and anything! Hungry to know at least how plants and fragrances and other things show in the chart,.

If you hate a particular plant it suggest that there is something in your psyche that the plant represents that your spirit hasn't come to terms with. IT c could even be linked with a karmic memory.

Lover's Influence
How will your lover influence your life?
A relationship can be transitory or permanent but it will leave its mark, its stain on the cloth of your life forever.

It is this permanent mark which the Synastry chart attempts to outline, it can draw a picture of that future. Of what will most likely happen if you stay with the man. Modern day astrologers seem to have forgotten this and they use synastry only as a method to determine compatibility or lack of it between two people.

Synastry is an old and complicated form of astrology that involves calculating and drawing up an astrological chart for you and then a chart for the other persons birth and carefully comparing it with you own, aspect by aspect. House by house, star by star, to see what kind of future there is. And what will come of the relationship. Its sorrows and its joys its shadows and summers, the portrait of the future are all outlined in the two charts like a picture. It is the element of mystery, the seeking of hidden knowledge that makes Synastry so attractive. The more we work on the chart the clearer the picture becomes and the more the future possibilities of our life show themselves from the shadows. All relationships from love to hate influence and reshape our lives. A Synastry need not be between lovers, it can be between any two people. Family members for example, or business partners,

This chapter outlines the first steps of Synastry, the most basic technique. You do not need to know much about astrology to follow it and learn from it, but you do need to have a copy of your Natal chart and a copy of your lovers Natal chart. If you do not have these you can find links later in the book to websites where you can create them.

Place the two charts side by side on your table; Your own chart represents you and your life, and your future. So we are going to use this chart as our base.

We begin with your first house. This is the house of the self the house of your personal life. What sign occupies your first house? Look for that sign in his chart, and see if he has any planet in that sign, if he does, we say that his planet is "in" your first house.

It is easiest to explain by example; Suppose you have Cancer in your first house, and only Cancer, no planets, no other signs. Then you look at his chart, you find the sign of cancer in it. Suppose he has Uranus in cancer in his chart, for this basic beginning, we look no further. It doesn't matter where or which house Uranus in cancer is in, in his chart, or what other aspects are made, we are keeping it very simple for now. So your chart is all that matters for the moment. So we find his Uranus is in your first house.

What this means is Your lover will have a "Uranian " influence over your personal life. The first house being your personal life. Uranus is a disruptive planet. So we could interpret this by saying " Your lover will have disruptive influence over your personal life.". Cancer is a sign that needs security, but Uranus is not a settled secure planet. So we Know the relationship may feel insecure. Cancer is the stomach and Uranus the " Nerves", so nervous stomach upsets induced by this relationship could be a problem for you. Uranus is excitement, and sudden events, the lovers influence is to bring excitement into a life that was secure and make it less secure   This is the beginning of   reading a Synastry

Now look to where each of his other planets fall in your chart, which of your houses do his planets fall in? Even using this basic scrap of Synastry that has been pared down to a simplified thread a lot can be told..

First House
Any of his planets falling in your first house will influence your private life. They will show your personal development or personal restrictions under him.

Lets take another example, if your lovers Saturn falls in your first house. Saturn is the planet of restriction, poverty, melancholy, ending, limitation, inhibition. So your personal life under such a man, many be less wealthy, more frugal, Your character may become restrained, inhibited enduring but withdrawn. Your body may become thinner because Saturn rules the skeleton and slimness. This is just a simple outline, the sign his Saturn and your first house share will modify the things I have written considerable, and also any aspects his Saturn to planets in your chart, but this is a basic beginning of learning to read the Synastry. The more you practice and the more you allow your intuition to flow the more detailed the picture you will drawn up for your client.

Second House
His planets being in your second house reveal how he

will influence your financial capacity. Financial help, or expenses you will occur due to the relationship are depicted here.; You don't want to see Neptune here, if you do, he might drain your income and bankrupt you, but of his Jupiter falls here, he will fill up your coffers to over flowing.

Third House

Any planets falling from hiss chart into your third house will reveal local travel and social activities together. His effect on your education Does he make you feel stupid or clever?;

Fourth House

This house will enlighten you about your home life with your soul mate. Will you be happy living together, is there some obstacle that prevents it. Where will you live?

Fifth House

This house is about affection or lack of it, the desire for children. How passionate or cold will the romance become.

Sixth House

Is your health helped or hindered by this relationship? Will it shred your nerves with anxiety? Will he pass on a sexually transmitted disease? He might if his Venus lands here. Will you become healthier in body and mind from knowing him, will he remain constant if your own health fails?

Seventh House

The house of marriage, it indicates how compatible you really are. If you marry Will you divorce? Will he remain faithful. Will you live happily ever after?

Eighth House

This house is about financial benefits through others. Will there be gain or loss through the lover? If you become a widow, will it be a wealthy one, or will the inheritance be pocketed by someone else.

Ninth House

Any of his planets sitting in your ninth house, house of the mind indicates the intellectual influence the lover will have over you. Planets in this house could also reflect his families attitude to you. The house of the " In laws" and journeys you make because of him. The better the planet the nicer the future together..

Tenth House

The tenth house rules your reputation, his planets here show how the relationship with your lover will affect your reputation. Will you be talked about? Will your name be ruined, brought into shame, if your soul mate is notorious will mud stick to you. Or will your reputation be improved. Remembering that your tenth house is also your Occupation, if you lover has any influence over this, it will also be displayed here. Will he force you to leave work after marriage? Will he be a tower of strength and support to your Career success?

Eleventh House

In the eleventh house the Synastry chart will indicate mutual acquaintances, friendships.

Twelfth House

Your lovers planet in the house of secrets, will uncover what is kept from view in the relationship, the workings that go on behind the scenes

Empty Houses

An empty house is a House of yours in which no planets of your lovers falls.. These are the rooms of your life that will remain unchanged by him. The spaces over which your lover will cast no great influence, but they are just as important in building up the whole picture of your love story

Reversing the Method

Once you have analyzed his influence on your life this way. You can use the same method in reverse. You can look at how your planets fall in his houses, and see what effect you will have on his life Will your Moon fall in his twelfth house, will you bring all his secrets into the light?. If your Moon is in cancer, then its his family secrets, in Virgo it may be hidden health problems your Moon brings out, and so. The Synastry from the two chart should form one picture..

In the other volumes we will go on to explore the art of Synastry some more. If you are new to chart comparison and impressed by this morsel of it, then imagine what wisdom a real comprehensive Synastry can reveal to you, where every plant, sign angle, aspect and star are counted, such complex work can only be admired, it can turn a crumb into a feast of such stupendous wealth.

Portrait Of A Lover.

People are endlessly interested in how a soul mates physical description, his face, his movements, his mannerisms can be drawn from the lines in a chart. This is what I specialize in. It is indeed a complex matter, and one where intuition and experience can help embellish the finer details. But the broad lines can always be drawn from a chart. In the previous book I illustrated how, here is some more of "how".

A simple line is to ask " Is the seventh house or a planet in it in the first or last degrees of a sign? The first and last degrees of any sign suggest the beginning of ending of a cycle. The cycle may be karmic, or personal. The sun n the first degree of its sign, or the seven house in the first degrees, suggest that the soul mate relationship or meeting will come at the time of a new cycle in your life.

The sun also rules lightness, brightness. He will lighten the complexion of hair. So that fore example if the sun is in Scorpio (traditionally a dark haired dark skinned sign) in the early degrees of the seventh, the partner will have lighter hair. and bright skin, so that instead of black hair and skin of dark honey, the soul mate would have brown hair and Ivory skin. The exact shade is determined by many chart aspects but this gives us a beginning.

If the sun is there, The soul mate will be someone who embodies the qualities of the sun. He will be young and fit for his age., strong and commanding or domineering in appearance. Someone bright and exhilarating and as stated previously the client will think inwardly he is very like true herself, a man who embody qualities of her soul twin. She will see all his characteristics in their best light.

Staying with the Scorpio sun, we know his character will seem reserved and serious. Some planets are tall some short, some young some old. Uranus generally increases the height so would the beginning degree, so if Uranus were aspecting our seventh house. We know he be a taller than the average. If Saturn also aspects not only would he be taller but rather thinner and shabbier because Saturn rules the skeleton, poverty, bones, death, misery all the " lean and mean things in life"

So already we have the beginning of a portrait here.

If the house or planet instead happened to be in the last degree it would suggest a soul mate met at the end of a cycle in life. The ending could be the end of previous relationship, end of ones youth, end of college,. always it will be individual ending to do with the rest of chart. So the picture Takes shape, we have Scorpio in the last degrees. A reserved quite man, met at time in life when something has ended or is ending. If Uranus aspects, then, a tall man. but not quite as tall as an earlier degree, so not the tallest of his race. But tallish. We then begin to sketch in hair, with the sun here his hair as we have said is brown. The exact degree will determine the exact shade. His skin is ivory or bamboo color, his skin is hot dry, non oily, we know this because of the sun. His eye color is dark amber, again our sun lightens the color, but if Uranus were aspecting the color would be mingled like the mingle shades in a stone, for Uranus is mixed colors.

Because of the sign we would expect his presence to have a hypnotic magnetism over others, but more warmth and charm or sparkle of manner than the average sinister Scorpio possesses because of the sun. We would expect him because of the sun to look healthy, to have an imposing regal,, proud, way of moving and standing,. The sun has vitality, so our man would not be a lethargic or a weak or wilting figure. But he would incorporate some of the other aspects into him, like Uranus, he may be clumsy, Like Scorpio, who seeks anonymity, he would not be aware of his imposing physique. And so on right through the chart we work to bring out its picture.

Astrology Chart reading is like embroidery we pick up a stitch here, and another there. I show you the shape of the pattern, and show you how the picture can be made, and then I leave it up to you to make your own garment, to look at other planets and think how this might show. Or what that might show, Some of you reading this will find it a frustrating method, but it is designed purely to make *you* think to draw on the depth of *your* inner knowledge, as well as mine.. This way you really truly learn and the spirit within you learns. If I simply gave a list of which aspects means blond hair; which mean a hooked nose and so on, you may knock out a reading with it, but you will learn nothing, except how to imitate or copy another persons work, and your own intuition will be crushed. What I do, like any Master, is give you the tools. I show you how to use them, and then what you make from it is entirely your own creation. A good teacher teaches you how to do his work, in your own way, not how to copy his work, but to take the skills of his work and to make something better and more dazzling of your own. He teaches you to be greater than the teacher, this way knowledge is transmitted and carried down through the generations and this is my hope for you my dearest student., That you will take what I have given you and carry it incorporating your own talent and using your own deductions and conclusions in your own unique and magnificent way

In each volume I will reveal more of the secrets of astrology to you, I can only teach you in same the way that I was taught. And if it works as well for you as it did for me then the flame of curiosity will be forever lit in your heart and the love of astrology will continue to walk with you down all the years of your life.

With each volume you have more than just a book, you have a system, a future knowledge, something that does have a price in money, but will live on within you, and you are the worlds future, you will carry the knowledge and the work forward. No book is ever as comprehensive as it could be, in this volume many things are not even touched on, the planet Chiron, the karmic Synastry of Soulmate. Our book is like a patchwork quilt of interesting things designed to make you think further, to give you a taste of delight but leave you hungering, and bets of all to bring out your own inner knowledge. Thus ends Volume two.

Find Ivarna online at;

http://www.ivarna.com

http://www.soulmate-japan.com (Japan

https://www.facebook.com/ivarna.kalinkova

www.ingramcontent.com/pod-product-compliance
Lightning Source LLC
Chambersburg PA
CBHW061946070426
42450CB00007BA/1067